Samuel Storey

To the golden Land

Sketches of a Trip to Southern California

Samuel Storey

To the golden Land
Sketches of a Trip to Southern California

ISBN/EAN: 9783337143909

Printed in Europe, USA, Canada, Australia, Japan

Cover: Foto ©ninafisch / pixelio.de

More available books at **www.hansebooks.com**

TO THE
GOLDEN LAND.

*SKETCHES
OF A TRIP TO SOUTHERN CALIFORNIA.*

ILLUSTRATED.

SAMUEL STOREY, M.P.

LONDON:
WALTER SCOTT, 24 WARWICK LANE,
PATERNOSTER ROW.
1889.

PREFACE.

THESE sketches were hastily penned amid the hurry of travel for publication in the *Newcastle Daily Chronicle*, the *Sunderland Daily Echo*, and certain other English newspapers. Complaisant friends have expressed a desire to have them in book form; therefore this volume appears.

If any of the public at large choose to buy it, they must take it for what it is worth.

I call Southern California the Golden Land, in part because for a generation we have drawn from it the most precious of metals, in part because when I left it its mountain sides and spreading *mesas* and sheltered valleys were covered with a golden efflorescence rich beyond compare.

To H. P., J. W. V., and F. G. S., my pleasant companions in many a glorious drive, I dedicate the volume. If it should please no one else, it will please them. And that will suffice

THE WRITER.

CONTENTS.

CHAPTER I.

HISTORIC GROUND—LOVELY WEATHER—OUR VOYAGE ACROSS—NEW YORK HARBOUR—AN ATHEIST AND A FISHERMAN—A PLEASANT INTERVIEW—SOMETHING FOR SMOKERS—BURNS THE SON OF THE TAVERN—WAS WASHINGTON A THIEF?—JONES TO THE RESCUE . . 7

CHAPTER II.

NEW YORK v. LONDON — BROADWAY — DOES WASHINGTON LIKE IT?—A HOMICIDAL HOTEL-KEEPER—THE ELEVATED RAILWAY—MERCURY THE GOD—THE POWER OF A FIVE-CENT PIECE—NEW YORK NEWSPAPERS—THE "TRIBUNE"—A TYPE-SETTING MACHINE WITHOUT TYPE—ELECTRICITY TO THE FRONT 12

CHAPTER III.

TO WASHINGTON BY TRAIN—A VISIT TO PRESIDENT CLEVELAND — REPUBLICAN SIMPLICITY — AN OBELISK INDEED—LINCOLN'S WINDOW—THE CAPITOL—FORD'S THEATRE—A TRAGIC ENDING 17

CHAPTER IV.

THE REBEL SOUTH—A REAL NEW YORKER—BLACK AND WHITE—HOME FROM MEETING—COLOURED LADIES AND GENTLEMEN—A NEW BIRMINGHAM AND A NEW SHEFFIELD—NEW YEAR'S DAY—NEW ORLEANS IN THE RAIN—MUD—A HUNT FOR PIOUS BLACKS—HARD ON THE WASHERWOMEN—ADIEU TO NEW ORLEANS . . 23

CHAPTER V.

AN EARTHLY PARADISE—THE WAY THITHER—DESERT—THE MIRAGE—JUST IN MEXICO—CITIES OF THE WEST—THE INDIAN IN PANTALOONS—LOS ANGELES—A MODEL HOME—IRISHMEN IN THE WEST—LAND SPECULATION—ADVERTISING EXTRAORDINARY 30

CHAPTER VI.

A STRANGE LAND—DULL GEOGRAPHY—A GREAT BRITAIN AND A HALF—MEN WANTED—WHO SHALL COME—THE SOUTH — PASADENA AND THE RAYMOND — SPANISH SAINTS—DRAWBACKS IN THE LAND—SUMMER AND ITS STRANGENESS—VINEYARDS—LUCKY BALDWIN—HEALTH QUESTIONS — LAND AND ITS PRICES — CHINEE CHEAP LABOUR—BOYCOTTING EVEN IN CALIFORNIA . . . 36

CHAPTER VII.

ODDS AND ENDS—GLADSTONE EVEN HERE—OFF TO RIVERSIDE—PROHIBITION CITIES—A SUNDAY MORNING SCENE—SOMETHING FOR THE CHILDREN—SAN DIEGO, THE CITY OF THE BAY—A PRESENT NAPLES; A FUTURE

CONTENTS.

LIVERPOOL—CLIMATE PAST COMPARE—A LOW DEATH-RATE—THE GREAT HOTEL—AN AMERICAN DIVES AND HIS CAR 45

CHAPTER VIII.

SAN DIEGO AND ITS BACK-COUNTRY—A USEFUL CHAMBER OF COMMERCE—A TRIP TO THE MOUNTAINS—DUTCHMEN TO THE FRONT—LOVELY EL CAJON—WATER SCHEMES—A SAIL BETWEEN SKY AND EARTH—CHINAMEN AND INDIANS—IN THE MOUNTAINS AT LAST—THE HIDDEN VALLEY—A CALIFORNIAN WEDDING—A MOUNTAIN SETTLEMENT—FALLBROOK—NOT EVEN A CORKSCREW ON PRINCIPLE—AN ALPINE SCENE IN THE LAND OF THE SUN . . 54

CHAPTER IX.

A MOUNTAIN SHEEP-RANCH—THE HAPPY VALLEY—RAIN—THE PALA MISSION—AN INDIAN CHIEF OF A NEW TYPE—THE GREAT MESA—COYOTES AT LAST—SCOTLAND AND CALIFORNIA—A GOLD FEVER AND ITS ISSUE—TYPICAL LAND SALE—AN OX ROASTED—ITS ROASTERS ROASTED TOO 64

CHAPTER X.

THE LAND BOOM AND ITS EFFECTS—LONDON ECLIPSED ON PAPER—WORK v. SPECULATION—SANTA BARBARA—A WESTERN RIVIERA—INTERVIEW WITH FRIARS OF ORDERS BROWN—THE OJAI VALLEY—A WONDROUS

WEATHER RECORD—STORM—BACK TO SAN DIEGO—MR.
ALBERT GREY—FINAL DRIVES—FLOWERS AND BIRDS
—ROAD-RUNNERS AND RATTLESNAKES—A HOMERIC
CONTEST—A COMMONPLACE ONE—HO FOR ENGLAND!
—MR. ALBERT GREY AT SEA 71

CHAPTER XI.

WESTERN NEWSPAPERS—THE "BOOM"—PAPERS AND THEIR
ODDITIES—AN UNIQUE ADVERTISEMENT—THE PARA-
GONS OF EDITORS—MR. POTT REDIVIVUS—O'BRIEN'S
HEAD OFF—PATTERN REPORTING—WESTERN HUMOUR
—OLD FOES MEET—SOMETHING FOR THE LAWYERS—
SOMETHING, TOO, FOR THE TEETOTALERS—THE LADIES
NOT FORGOTTEN—A COSTLY COFFIN—A MODEL WIFE
—SULPHUR SAM'S WARNING 81

CHAPTER XII.

3500 MILES IN THE TRAIN—PITTSBURGH—WASHINGTON—
MR. BLAINE—THE AMERICAN NAVY—PRESIDENT HAR-
RISON—WASHINGTON'S HOME—NEW YORK—HOMEWARD
BOUND 93

ILLUSTRATIONS.

	PAGE
MAP	
MR. BLAINE	7
PRESIDENT CLEVELAND	16
JOHN BROWN'S SONS AT HOME	21
HOMES IN LOS ANGELES	30
BOUNDARY STONE BETWEEN CALIFORNIA AND MEXICO	33
PASADENA	39
FAC-SIMILE OF ESSAY BY A CHINESE COOK	45
AVENUE AT RIVERSIDE	47
ORANGE GROVES	48
ORANGE PACKING	50
HOTEL ON CORONADA BEACH	53
CARTING LUMBER FOR THE FLUME	55
THE GREAT FLUME	57
VIADUCT ON THE FLUME	59
TUNNEL IN THE FLUME	61
A JACK-RABBIT DRIVE	63
SANTA ROSA	65
A CALIFORNIAN ROSE-BUSH	71
SANTA BARBARA MISSION	75
THE IRISH MONK	77
WINTER BATHING IN THE PACIFIC	80
AN ADOBÉ DWELLING	84
SAN GABRIEL MISSION	87
PRESIDENT HARRISON	92
MOUNT VERNON, WASHINGTON'S HOME	94
THE BED AND ROOM WHERE WASHINGTON DIED	96
WASHINGTON'S TOMB	98

MR. BLAINE.

TO THE GOLDEN LAND.

CHAPTER I.

HISTORIC GROUND—LOVELY WEATHER—OUR VOYAGE ACROSS—
NEW YORK HARBOUR—AN ATHEIST AND A FISHERMAN—
A PLEASANT INTERVIEW—SOMETHING FOR SMOKERS—BURNS
THE SON OF THE TAVERN—WAS WASHINGTON A THIEF?—
JONES TO THE RESCUE.

On the Railway,
December 31st, 1888.

I AM passing over the historic ground where many of the early battles of the Great War were fought. I left Washington at 11.24 A.M., and have just run through Manassas Junction and the cuttings where the first fight of Bull Run took place. The country is rough, undulating, and wooded. Looking at it, one realises how tough, hand-to-hand, and incomplete the fighting must necessarily have been, especially between armies not yet highly disciplined. It is a region calculated to fill soldiers with unknown fears, and generals with indecision. I hope to reach New Orleans, 1147 miles, on the morning after to-morrow, spend my New Year's Day there, and then go on to Los Angeles, 2000 miles farther. It seems a stiff business, but a luxurious cushioned chair in a palace-car by day and a comfortable bed in the sleeper at night minimise one's pains. Besides, the day is lovely. Imagine one of the brightest Christmas Days you ever saw, with blue sky, gentle wind, and a keen appetising air with just a suspicion of frost in it, and you have the weather I am revelling in. I wonder what yours is like?

Having so introduced myself, let me turn back and begin at the beginning. Of our voyage across I need not say much. It began in sunshine at Queenstown, and ended in sunshine at New York; and if in the interim we had stormy seas and much rolling and tossing, still I stood to my guns—in other words, I punctually presented myself at every meal, which was more than three-quarters of the passengers did, the list of absentees including one gentleman who had crossed forty-seven times. Reflecting on the facts, I proudly feel that in my person Britannia still rules the waves. We steamed into New York harbour on the sunny morning of the day before Christmas. I had, in view of my oft-intended but never-till-now-realised visit, so steeped myself in descriptive accounts of the scene opening before me that it seemed strangely familiar. The New Jersey highlands; the low-lying tongue of Sandy-Hook; the magnificent statue of Liberty; the massive Brooklyn Bridge; the historic Battery Point where the Governors lived when we English ruled the land, and at no great distance from which George Washington was sworn in as First President of the United States; the rapid Hudson; the wharves; the gorgeous river steamers, and the swift-plying ferries—all were before me. No need to descend to detail. Many of my friends have seen New York from the sea, but never one of them on a lovelier day than I.

The revenue boat brought off for me a welcoming telegram from my friend Andrew Carnegie. By 4 P.M. I had landed; and that night I slept once again in a Christian bed instead of a bunk. My Christmas Day I spent with Mr. Carnegie's family party; but the interesting event of the day to me was the visit I paid to Colonel Ingersoll. Let me confess. There are only two New Yorkers I really was curious to see. I am not much interested in the merchant princes, the millionaires, or the politicians of the Empire State. And I may probably be thought a little odd in my tastes. But the two men I wished to see were the above-named Apostle of Agnosticism and W. C. Prime, author of *I Go A-Fishing*, the raciest fisherman's book published since gossiping, inimitable Izaak Walton died. The latter (Prime, not Walton) I am to meet as I return; one o'clock saw Mr. Carnegie and me at the door of the other. He lives in a handsome house, No. 400 Fifth Avenue, and received us in his library. "Colonel Bob," as he is familiarly called, had with him his wife and daughter, and, as he rose with a cheery face, presented the spectacle of a stout, large-framed man, with massive head and face, a merry twinkle in the eye, and a gently satirical mouth. Colonel Ingersoll may be described as the Bradlaugh of America, just as honest, just as persistently wrong theologically (so most of us believe); less self-assertive, more cultured, physically and facially of the same type. And, like Bradlaugh, he is fortunate in a daughter. A more charming, graceful, and gracious-mannered American girl it would be impossible to see. In any assemblage of fair women Miss Ingersoll would be notable. Strange, is it not, that these unbelieving heathen should be blessed with heaven's choicest gifts! We had a pleasant hour's talk. Carnegie and Ingersoll—both good talkers—made an interesting couple, the small Scotchman with his Napoleonic head, and the massive American, whose shoulders seemed made to push mountains from his path. The two reminded one of Tom Hood's couplet—

> "The big judge and the little judge,
> The judges of a(s)size."

Religion and theology, by common consent, were eschewed. We talked of tobacco. Ingersoll was smoking a fragrant Havannah. He puffed and plunged into praise of the divine weed. If he believe in nothing else he believes in tobacco. He rolled out to us a little eulogy he had contributed to a new work on Cuba, his voice modulated in curious rhythmic cadences. It was poetic, though not in rhyme. The thing itself I hope to get for my friends, for I have written to its author for a copy, but the inimitable delivery of it I cannot reproduce. We talked of Burns, of whom the Colonel and his daughter are passionately fond. "How odd," said he, "that such gifts of genius should have been bestowed on a son of the tavern and not on a son of the church!" Then we fell on the great war. Carnegie and Ingersoll revelled in reminiscences. The former began the recital of a great scene of which the latter was the hero; but the hero himself broke in, and with humorous energy took up the tale. It was in the early days of the war. Emancipation and the duty of the North thereon had become a burning question; but men were slow to cross the Rubicon, for they knew that a policy of emancipation involved war to the knife. It was necessary for some bold man to speak out. A great meeting was held at Chicago, and Colonel Bob was invited to speak. "Fellow-citizens," he began, "if a man appropriates a saw or any other implement of labour, we call him a thief. What shall we call the man who appropriates the labourer, the producer of the implement? *He is a thief, too.*" The bold pronouncement was reported and repeated over all the North amidst acquiescent applause; it was received with anger and execration in the South.

A little while after Ingersoll had to speak just on the borderland between the belligerent States. It was in a place where Confederate sympathisers were almost as numerous as Federals. There was an immense meeting, and all the indications pointed to—in vulgar parlance—a row. No shrinking would avail. It was necessary to take that bull by the horns. Colonel Bob began amid mingled cheers and groans:—"Fellow-citizens, I said in Chicago if a man appropriates to himself another man's saw or implement of labour we call him a thief. If a man appropriates the labourer, the producer of the saw, he is a thief too. (Dead silence.) Fellow-citizens, what I said in Chicago I say here. He *is* a thief!" A mingled burst of yells and groans and cheers, and an ugly rush. One man roared out—"George Washington owned slaves. Was *he* a thief?" "The gentleman asks me was Washington a thief?" retorted Ingersoll, straightening himself up, and in tones of thunder—"*Yes, sir, by God*

HE WAS." Then in his drollest, driest tones, and with a twinkling eye fixed on his angry questioner, he added—"Does the gentleman want my opinion about any other individual?" There was a momentary pause, then a burst of hilarious laughter, and Colonel Bob went on triumphantly to the end.

But hold, my space fails, just as time failed that pleasant afternoon. Regretfully we took our leave, Colonel Bob begging me cordially to call and see him again when I returned to New York. I promised; but dare I? For at my hotel I happened to alight on a choice extract from a recent sermon by the Rev. Sam Jones, revivalist and buffoon. It presents another view of Colonel Bob, and my readers can have it as dessert after lunch :—"That blatant, blab-tongued fool. Why, a fly can sit on his nose and kick him in both eyes, and he wouldn't know it. Bob has no brains, for he can see through a gimlet hole with both eyes to oncet. Agnostics an' fools—if they want to be so, let 'em set an' fan themselves with their ears."

CHAPTER II.

New York *v.* London—Broadway—Does Washington like it?—A Homicidal Hotel-Keeper—The Elevated Railway—Mercury the God—The Power of a Five-Cent Piece—New York Newspapers—The "Tribune"—A Type-setting Machine without Type—Electricity to the Front.

On the Railway, January 2nd, 1889.

I SPENT my second day in New York in making myself amply acquainted with its topography. It is by no means my intention to burden others with details of all I saw and heard. I shall simply pull the plums out of the pudding, and if they prove to be not very toothsome, the more's the pity.

I began at the bottom, or south end of the island. New York, as all America knows, is surrounded by water, its island-bounds extending fourteen miles north and south, and from one and a half miles to two and a half miles east and west. Within this confined space more than a million "free and independents" live and work or idle or speculate or thieve or beg. But the population has, so to say, spilt over into neighbouring islands and the mainland, and altogether there are nearer three millions than one gathered within metropolitan limits. The rate of growth is enormous. London is much bigger than New York to-day, but it is quite an open question whether one hundred, or even fifty years hence, the relative positions may not be reversed.

I began at the bottom of Broadway, which is not broad, and is disgracefully paved, its sideways disfigured with ugly telegraph poles, and its roadways inundated with tramcars. It is full, however, of fine buildings and handsome shops. This backbone of the city should have run due north, but it trends steadily to the nor'-nor'-west, and may be described as a backbone gone astray among the ribs. On either side of it are the main avenues, really running north and south, and some of which necessarily cross Broadway at an acute angle. The streets run at right angles to these avenues, and by the time you have got from No. 1 Street to No. 150 you have done a pretty piece of walking. Gazed at from a balloon above, the city must look like nothing so much as a huge gridiron.

Down from the balloon, however, let us come. Wander on with me among the busy, surging crowds, and meander ever and anon into the side streets. Here is famous Wall Street, where more speculation takes place in a day than in any other equal space in the world. There, from the steps of the U.S. Treasury, George Washington's statue looks calmly down on the scheming crowds of citizens, for the honesty of all of whom the pure-souled, unselfish Father of the Commonwealth would scarcely care to go bail. It is little more than a century since he stood on this very spot in the flesh and was sworn in as First President of a new nation of two millions of men. Now there are seventy millions of them. A century hence who can say how many there may be? Let us on, pausing at Union Square and Madison Square, where there is at any rate one statue of admirable design —that of Admiral Farragut. We look in at the enormous store where the famous Tiffany displays his myriad gauds of gold and silver and jewels, and lunch at Hoffman's, whose proprietor shot the notorious James Fisk, did his ten years, and now lunches and dines the fashionable crowds in palatial rooms. The only comment some practical New Yorkers made on that catastrophe was— ·What a pity Fisk also did not shoot his shooter!

Now, if your lunch has refreshed you enough, look there to your left, where one block off an ugly, unadorned platform crosses the street. That is the elevated railway—a noticeable feature of the city; ugly beyond dreams, but oh! so useful. How New Yorkers could get about over the disgracefully-paved streets without it man knows not. There are four such lines, all beginning at the bottom of Broadway, and two of them trending to the west and two to the east till they reach their appointed track; and then all four stretch out due north for miles along the avenues. They are reared in the centre of the roadways upon square balks of timber high enough for loaded vehicles to pass under. The trains run over them from early morn to late midnight. Each day they pour tens, hundreds of thousands into the business limits, and each evening speed them out again. If you are fanciful you may compare New York to a sandglass, with a huge bulb at one end, connected by four elongated necks with as many bulbs at the other end, the whole concern "run," or "operated," so the jargon goes here, by swift-winged Mercury, who is, I believe, the god of trading, as I am certain he is of thieving. Every morning the waggish god turns his glass on its single bulb, and the black-coated human atoms pour madly down through the narrow necks of the "elevated" into the vortex, where he stirs them about and worries them all day long. Then at five o'clock he reverses his glass, and away pour the atoms again—out, out to their virtuous homes to tell of money made or lost, some by honest work, some by legal trade, and some by well-veneered rascality.

For a ride on the elevated, long or short, you pay five cents. Many things in the States cost this magic trifle. We are taught in England that a dollar equals fifty pence of our money. According to my present experience, its purchasing power is little more than that of a shilling with us. Your morning paper is five cents (2½d.), a cigarette five cents, a box of wax-lights five cents, "shine your boots" five cents, a pair of shoe-laces five cents, an orange five cents, a glass of beer five cents; even the beggars, of whom I have found not a few, both in New York and elsewhere, ask, not for a penny, but a nickel—

i.e., five cents. A cup of tea costs fifteen or twenty cents, according to the fancy of the seller; a modest lunch seventy cents; a cab to the station a dollar and a half; a porter looks disgusted if he gets less than a quarter. They have a playful little habit, too, of soaring above the giving of change. I sent a telegram the other day. It cost 148 cents. I handed in 150. No balance was handed back, and it is "mean" to ask for your own. Silver was little accounted of in the days of Solomon, and cents (less than five) don't count here. Glorious home of freedom!

Of one pleasant and enlightening visit during my peregrinations I must not forget to tell. Naturally I am interested in the newspapers. New York is full of them. The *Herald*, of course, enjoys world-wide fame; and the *World*, under the guidance of my friend Mr. Pulitzer, has achieved a sudden success only equalled in recent days by the wondrous growth of the London *Star*. All, however, are good, enterprising, bright—if a hypercritical Briton may be allowed to say so—too bright. Good fortune threw me across Mr. Hart Lyman, one of the principals of the literary staff of the *Tribune*, the great Republican organ of Democratic New York. And I availed myself of his courteous offer to examine the inner workings of that mighty organ. Of much—the machines, the telegraphic and telephonic and literary arrangements, etc., etc.—I need not speak. We can equal these at home. But imagine my surprise when, on entering the composing-room, I found—*no type*. None; except a very limited quantity of large, odd sizes. How, then, is the paper set? By electrical machines.

There they stood in a row, thirty grim, silent demons. At the turning of a little handle they are instantaneously full of life. Each has a key-board like a piano, and in front of the operator a series (105 in number) of oblong tubes, like the attenuated reeds of a miniature organ. These hollow tubes are about two feet in length, as broad internally as type is high, and with a frontage as large as the type is thick. Each is fitted with brass squares, with a section cut out so as to leave the shape thus—

Each letter has its own series of nicks on the inner edges of the V; and there is a square-edged space at the side where is the matrix, or reverse of the letter. The operator, sitting with the copy before him, touches the keys, and each letter falls in due order till the line is complete. Two steel fingers seize this, push it along, space it, and justify it. Again two fingers seize it and push it in front of a little cistern full of molten lead. As it reaches its place the machine pushes out from the cistern a layer of lead line-long and type-thick. The faces of the cooling lead and the brass edge come into contact, the matrix letters are impressed as positives on the lead, and there remains a solid line of type. This goes in due course to the galley, and the columns and pages are made up and stereotyped in the ordinary way. Meanwhile the machine whisks the brasses up to a series of little waggons, running on an endless wire above the tubes, and as each brass reaches its own nicks it drops into its tube, and is ready again for use. It has only been out of its nest one-third of a minute at the utmost. As a consequence few brasses are needed. The letter oftenest used, e, has only sixteen. I could carry the whole complement for a machine in my coat pockets. "And what will a machine perfect?" said I. "One machine with one man only will set five thousand ems an hour," said Mr. Lyman, "and do its own distributing. And there is no waste of type, no wear and tear. It is equal to six men." "Do other papers use it?" "None in New York; a few in the country, where they don't compete with us, and are owned by our friends." "And England?" "None in England, *as yet*."

Bad news this for compositors, eh? Not a bit of it, my friends. I saw a copy of the *Tribune* the other day of twenty-four full pages! The introduction of electrical setting will only end in making existing papers bigger and fuller of interest to the public, whilst it will make new papers possible in scores of places where now they can't be made to pay.

PRESIDENT CLEVELAND.

CHAPTER III.

TO WASHINGTON BY TRAIN—A VISIT TO PRESIDENT CLEVELAND
— REPUBLICAN SIMPLICITY — AN OBELISK INDEED — LIN-
COLN'S WINDOW—THE CAPITOL—FORD'S THEATRE—A TRAGIC
ENDING.

In the Train, January 3rd, 1889.

SATISFIED with a brief present visit to New York, of which I shall probably see more as I return, I was driven on Friday to the Railway Station, was ferried across the Hudson, and found myself on the cars in Jersey City, bound for Washington, with letters of introduction to the President and his secretary, Colonel Lamont. Washington is about 240 miles from New York. You pay 27s. for the ticket, and 14s. extra for the Pullman Palace Car on the Limited Express. The road hugs the coast more or less, passing through Trenton, Philadelphia, and Baltimore. I cannot say that this is an interesting journey. You pass mainly through a cultivated and prosperous country, but there are stretches of low waste, and you miss the comfortable-looking farm steadings, the trim hedges, and the well-kept ditches which give large areas of England the aspect of a cultivated garden.

Trenton was interesting to me historically, for it was there that Washington sustained his most disastrous defeat in (from the American standpoint) the darkest days of the Revolutionary War—a defeat nobly and speedily redeemed by victories at Germantown and Brandywine, just over the rolling hills to the south-west. Philadelphia, with its 800,000 Pennsylvanians, and Baltimore, the seaport and capital of Maryland, I cannot describe, for our stay was of the briefest. Leaving New York at 10 A.M., we steamed into the depôt at Washington a little after 4 P.M. —good travelling, though, as will be noted, you have to pay fifty per cent. excess to secure it. I first saw Washington on a lovely December day. The westering sun was sinking in glory among the distant hills, and its last rays lit up the marble pillars and mighty dome of the Capitol, the Parliament House of nearly forty free united states, each of which in far distant cities, in some cases beyond Alpine ranges or desert wastes, has its own Parliament and its own Executive administering its own State affairs. Note this fact, please; find the moral of it for yourselves.

Washington may be honestly described as a fine city. Its main avenue, as wide as four ordinary streets, is asphalted; tramcar lines occupy its centre; its sidewalks are adorned with trees, and many of the buildings are noble. It stretches east and west for a mile and a half. At the east end is the Capitol, seated on the swelling crest of a low hill; at the west end is the famous White House, the official residence of the successive Presidents of the United States. The surrounding avenues, streets, and squares are planned and laid out in the magnificent American way, to satisfy the needs of a population of a million; but at present the city contains less than a quarter of that number. Its planners meant that it should radiate in every direction from the Capitol hill, the better buildings running away eastward. But cities, like pigs, will not be driven. The citizens have eschewed the goodly sites in the east, filled up the swamps west and north-west, and thither Washington grows.

Advanced as the day was, I called on Colonel Lamont, but, finding he was out driving, had to content myself with leaving my letters. In a couple of hours, however, a messenger arrived from him with a note, whose republican simplicity merits its reproduction here—

"*Executive Mansion, Washington, Dec.* 28, 1888.

"DEAR SIR,—If you call at ten o'clock to-morrow morning I shall find great pleasure in introducing you to the President.

Very truly yours,

DANIEL A. LAMONT."

No ridiculous etiquette! No punctilious delay! He never asked me whether I had a coat-of-arms, or had secured the right sort of cocked hat, and the proper kind of velvet breeches! At ten next morning, accordingly,

I walked across to the White House, which literally glistened in the bright sunlight. It had a pleasant, kindly look—the look of a great English country house of the better sort; for the Americans do not lodge their chief in a palace, but a home. It stands on the same foundations as the older house which we English burnt down during our second war with America in 1814, and its double front looks on one side to the north upon a broad boulevard, and on the other over sloping gardens to the mighty Potomac. No long array of flunkeys loafed around; an usher simply attired, like a man, not like a pantaloon, received my card and passed me upstairs, where another official, similarly attired, ushered me into a room, and sent for Colonel Lamont. That gentleman speedily made his appearance, informed me that the President would be at liberty "quite soon," and begged me to be seated. The room, he informed me, was known as the Cabinet Room, where the President was in the habit of meeting his Cabinet in council, for in this country the Chief of the State actively takes part in the Government, and is chief in more than name.

Whilst we pleasantly talked, a door on the right opened to emit the Attorney-General, and in a moment the Colonel had ushered me in, and I was face to face with the President. Thus simply and without parade is one man (however petty) in this democratic land introduced to another, though he be President over sixty millions of men. It was the first time I had ever stood immediately in presence of a live Chief Ruler. I once saw a dead one. To meet one thus as gentleman meets gentleman was at once a pride and a pleasure; but knee-scraping and hand-kissing one's soul abhors. My democratic vertebræ are not supple enough for that nonsense.

President Cleveland sat at a writing-table drawn into a large window, and rose as I entered, saying courteously, "Good-morning." "This is my first visit to the States, Mr. President," I replied, "and I felt it would be at once a duty and a pleasure to pay my respects to the Chief of the State." "You are heartily welcome; pray be seated."

Mr. Cleveland is a short, stout man, with a large face, and a large head only partially covered with hair. A heavy moustache adorns his upper lip. He gives you an impression of solidity, but by no means of stolidity. Do not expect me to give the details of our half-hour's interview. Be sure there were two subjects we eschewed. He never mentioned the burning Sackville incident, and I was too discreet to make any reference to his own recent defeat at the polls. The only political matter we touched was that of International Arbitration. He told me he had received with great pleasure the recent deputation of English M.P.'s, and had been much struck with their evident earnestness in a great cause. Drawing me then into the bow-window he pointed out to me the Potomac, and over it the rolling plains and hills of fair Virginia. I asked if this was Lincoln's room. No. Mr. Lincoln liked the office. I should see it. There, in front of us, on the other side of the river, rose Washington's monument. Talk of obelisks! Cleopatra's Needle is a baby to this. It is sixty-three feet square at the base, and tapers upwards till its point challenges the clouds at a height of 550 feet, whilst our Needle in London is, I believe, somewhat over 100 feet. Its hollow interior contains a lift, by which the practical Americans whisk you comfortably to the top if you are so inclined. "I've got that finished anyhow," said Mr. Cleveland. "When I came here first I felt it odd to have it frowning down on me; but in four years I have learned to think of it as a friend, and many a time I turn from my papers and watch its varying hues under the changing skies." "A friend indeed," said I, "if Washington's spirit hovers round it."

Enough of this gossip. Our talk was interesting to me, but might not be to others. The Senator for Arkansas was announced (for this poor ruler is seldom allowed to be idle), and I took my leave, the President cordially shaking hands and wishing me "a good time" and better health in California. Colonel Lamont awaited me, and under his guidance I entered the "office." There was

JOHN BROWN'S SONS AT HOME.

Lincoln's favourite window, there his desk, nay, there stood an old framed chair, just such as you see in American kitchens, painted a bright, ugly red, the paint chipped and worn and scraped off here and there. May not imagination body forth the "rail-splitter" working away in his rough west-country chair? How much was on the hazard! Have you read the moving history of those eventful days of March and April 1861? Lincoln had just been inducted into his high office, and stood in the White House, chief of a riven State. The South was in open rebellion; its armies were mustering. He had no soldiers. The telegraph indeed brought news of the rising in the North, the musterings in New York and Philadelphia, the march of the volunteers southward. But Baltimore stood on the railway track, and Baltimore, much inclined to be rebel, refused to let the volunteers past. Then the wires were cut, and Lincoln stood unguarded, isolated from the faithful North, face to face with the rebel South; almost alone, but firm as adamant, true as steel. Tidings at last came through that the troops had been sent by sea and would sail up the Potomac.

Every morning Lincoln hurried to his favourite window; his yearning eyes searched the southern horizon for the sails that did not appear. Before him rolled the famous river; immediately beyond it all was rebel ground. There, on his right, but hidden by the hills, is Harper's Ferry, where John Brown struck the first open downright blow at slavery. At an equal distance to the left, sheltered by those trees, lie the bones of the Father of the Republic. In front there, just six miles off, where the tall chimneys rise, is Alexandria, held by the advance troops of the Confederate army. Here, close to the right, rises over the trees the white façade of Arlington, the ancestral home of the Lees, whence General Robert had ridden south to command the rebel armies, and lead them in many a fierce and fratricidal fight. Still the ships come not. It seems as though President, Cabinet, and Capitol are at the mercy of any adventurous foe. At last, in his anxiety, Lincoln was seen to lean his weary brow against the window-frame; and as his fingers impatiently tapped the panes he muttered again and again, "Will they never come?" I protest it is one of the pathetic scenes of history; the most pathetic scene (save the last) in Lincoln's own mournfully-victorious career!

From the White House I passed to the Capitol. What has been so oft described need not be described by me. The building, in a word, externally and internally, is magnificent, and worthy of a mighty people. The chambers in which the two Houses meet are more spacious than ours in London, and the arrangements for the public just as commodious as ours are the reverse. Congress was not in session, but sundry representatives of the people were lounging on their seats, and comfortably enjoying their cigars within the sacred precincts. Every nation has ways of its own.

Weary though I was, I availed myself of the last hour of daylight to find Tenth Street and Ford's Theatre, where, on Good Friday, 1865, Lincoln was foully slain by Booth. The theatre is now used as a Government museum. No place for Mimic Tragedy here henceforth for ever. I traced the route by which the assassin, mounting his horse, made his way over the Long Bridge and so into Virginia, there in brief space to meet a murderer's doom. Opposite the theatre is the house where his friends, horror-stricken, speechless, bore the wounded President. And there he breathed his life out, speaking never again. A plain tablet on the wall bears the simple inscription—

In this House
ABRAHAM LINCOLN DIED,
April 16, 1865.

Invited, I entered the house and passed into the room built on at the back—a low, two-windowed chamber, half-filled by the bed when it stood there to receive its tragic load. I stood with bowed and reverent head pondering the dire catastrophe. To me that spot was holy ground, for a patriot-martyr died there!

CHAPTER IV.

THE REBEL SOUTH—A REAL NEW YORKER—BLACK AND WHITE—HOME FROM MEETING—COLOURED LADIES AND GENTLEMEN—A NEW BIRMINGHAM AND A NEW SHEFFIELD—NEW YEAR'S DAY—NEW ORLEANS IN THE RAIN—MUD—A HUNT FOR PIOUS BLACKS—HARD ON THE WASHERWOMEN—ADIEU TO NEW ORLEANS.

In the Train, January 4th, 1889.

THERE are various routes by rail from Washington to New Orleans. I chose the shortest, the Piedmont Air Line; so called, first because it runs at the foot of the Blue Mountains, and secondly because it cuts straight as a bee-line across the country. You pass through the States of Virginia, North Carolina, South Carolina Georgia, Alabama, and Mississippi, the heart of what was the Rebel South. I saw the land at its worst, for the cotton and maize crops were gathered, and the fields looked empty, burnt-up, and unkempt. The ugliness was redeemed, however, by low rolling hills, covered with timber, and ever and anon the passage of a river opened up views of rich and verdant valleys. The country does not look to be thickly inhabited, and indeed is not so. It was my fortune to meet upon the train a New York gentleman, who fell into easy conversation. This Mr. Buckley is a typical Northern American, tall, sprucely-dressed, intelligent, travelled, and well-read. He is director of one of the New York banks, director too of the Brooklyn dry-docks, owner of a cotton plantation in Carolina, and of coal-mines somewhere else; finally, chief shareholder in one of the great railroads running west from St. Louis to California. Under his guidance I left the gorgeous palace-car and crossed over the gangway into the general car, and then into the smoking-car beyond.

The general cars in the States are essentially democratic. There the people sat, male and female, rich and poor, black and white together. I was in the midst of negro-land, and of course in the company of many good Democrats. This "black question" is not settled yet. There is much race jealousy and hatred, often rising into blood-shedding on both sides, though mainly on the side of the whites. One Democrat suggested that things would never be right till there was a bloody racial war. You see the blacks will persist in multiplying, *will* insist that the American Constitution is right in declaring that all men are free and equal. Another Democrat thought that the blacks should be driven or deported bodily out of the land. I suggested that the whites brought them there, and should bear the ills their greed created. He did not see that. Yet another was of opinion that at any rate they should have no votes since they did not know what they voted about. As if all whites did—here or elsewhere! I mildly suggested schools, inter-marriage, and patience, and he looked at me as though I were dangerous.

At one station a crowd of what Lord Salisbury might fairly describe as "black people" got into the car. There were some fifty or sixty of them, the men in black or dark clothes, with white shirts, and the inevitable wide-awake hat; the women, some of them nicely and neatly dressed, others in garments and hats of fearful colours and wonderfully made. They laughed and chattered and ate oranges and apples just like your even Christian. The young folk made eyes (such eyes) at one another; the elder men dandled the babies. They were mostly jet black, but here and there paler faces indicated the marriage of races. A jovial crew. They had been at a religious meeting (would I had been there!), and were on their way to their cabin-homes; poor things, sir, but their own. I did not hear one rude, foul, or offensive word. All was mirth and kindliness; and when they left us the men helped the women and bairns as carefully out of the car as though they had been English gentlemen. "Isn't that a better use to put them to than making slaves of them?" I suggested to my Democratic friends; but I don't think they saw even that.

At one part of our journey we skirted the coal and iron district of Northern Alabama, Georgia, and Southern Tennessee. Enormous quantities of these precious minerals are being opened up in this part of the South, mainly by Northern enterprise and capital; and the effect upon the prosperity of the district has been marked. The population is increasing by leaps and bounds, and a new Birmingham and a new Sheffield have arisen which bid fair to rival their prototypes in the old land. The coal and iron lie close together. This is seldom so in America. For instance, I think I have heard Mr. Carnegie say that he brings some of his iron ore 1200 miles by rail. English manufacturers will understand what that means. But here the ores are side by side, and furnaces and coal-pits combine to make the landscape hideous and the people rich. Along with manufacturing has come the true American itch for Protection. The growth of this desire lost Cleveland much support in these parts. Democrats ratted to Harrison. It would be odd now if, not education and the negro, but coal and iron broke up the Solid South.

The second morning brought us to Atlanta, a populous and thriving city of some 80,000 souls and the capital of Georgia. It was here that Sherman routed utterly the Southern forces, capturing the city and its military stores in that famous march through Georgia which broke the back of the Confederacy. By the way, I have mentioned the Confederates and the War so often that I may not inappropriately weave in a little incident here. The Confederate States (as all know—many to their cost) issued paper-money, each bill proudly bearing on its face, "The Confederate States of America promise to pay —— dollars." They never did pay, never will. They are not; Grant took them. Now, a certain enterprising firm in

Savannah held a number of these notes after the war, and knowing nothing better to do with them, printed the Lament of some Southern Poet on the back, stamped their own trade-stamp in front as an advertisement, and retailed them at a trifling charge. One for five dollars came to my hands. Admire the Lament of

THE CONFEDERATE BILL.

Representing nothing on God's earth now,
   And naught in the waters below it,
As the pledge of a nation that passed away,
   Keep it, dear friend, and show it.

Show it to those who will lend an ear
   To the tale this trifle will tell:
Of liberty born of a patriot's dream,
   Of a storm-cradled nation that fell.

Too poor to possess the precious ores,
   And too much of a stranger to borrow;
We issued to-day our promise to pay,
   And hoped to redeem on the morrow.

The days rolled on, and the weeks became years,
   But our coffers were empty still;
Gold was so scarce that the treasury quaked
   If a dollar should drop in the till.

But the faith that was in us was strong indeed,
   Though our poverty will be discerned,
And this little cheque represents the pay
   Our suffering veterans earned.

We knew it had scarcely a value in gold,
   Yet as gold our soldiers received it;
It gazed in our eyes with a promise to pay,
   And every true soldier believed it.

But our boys thought little of price or pay,
   Of the bills that were all overdue;
We knew if it bought us our bread to-day,
   'Twas the best our poor country could do.

Keep it—it tells our history o'er,
   From the birth of the dream to the last;
Modest and born of the Angel Hope,
   Like our hope of success—it passed.

At Atlanta I saw the first sign of the cloven foot in respect of the treatment of the negro. There are three waiting-rooms at the station—one for ladies, one for gents (not gentlemen), and one for "coloured people." The railway companies thus bend to local prejudice when it costs them next to nothing. When it is a question of providing separate cars, however, which would cost much, economy slays prejudice, and, as I have noted, the lion and the lamb lie down together.

All day and all night we drivelled along through Alabama and Mississippi, passing through Montgomery and Mobile; through the latter just after the New Year had come into the world. The city was all alight, the citizens firing off squibs and crackers in honour of 1889. It was odd to lie in one's bed, comfortably propped up on the pillows, and gaze through the windows at the shadowy land; sometimes dashing through dreary cane-brakes, then into the obscurity of dense forests, and anon over wide, misty, watery wastes of grim bayous. At length at seven o'clock on the third morning we steamed into New Orleans, and amidst pouring rain I made my way to the Hotel St. Charles. When it rains in the Crescent City it *does* rain. If I tell you little of New Orleans you must blame that rain for it. I had planned but a brief stay of twenty-four hours, and was not tempted to extend my visit. The city, standing on the left bank of the mighty Mississippi, so poetically known to the Indians as Father of Waters, is built on the mud left by the river. It is inhabited by a mixed population of Americans, French, Spanish, negroes, and Chinese. Many of its buildings are fine, and its streets spacious. The main street, Canal, is long and straight, and 200 feet wide, with a double row of trees in the centre; then lines of tramways, then a roadway on either side, and finally broad flagged sidewalks, sheltered by arcades, which the shopkeepers are allowed to run out. The footpaths are thus smooth and dry even on the wettest day. But the pavements! oh, Heavens! Canal Street is paved with stone blocks planted on the mud, and twelve inches square. Anything smaller would, they say, sink away through the mud. Why not, I suggested, sink the pavement twelve inches for a base, put in macadam, and asphalte the top? The answer was, the city could not afford it. Think of it. A city with 300,000 people can't afford to make its main street decently passable. Cab-riding is a series of dislocations, and as for crossing on foot in wet weather—well, the only way is to double up your trousers and plunge in; you may come out, or you may not. I tell you these Americans are so busy making dollars that they have no time to make comfort. It is so nearly everywhere. In my infinite compassion for their state, I wished then and there that I could send out to them my friend Alderman B——. He would mend their ways in six months, or more probably die of a broken heart in the meantime.

New Year's Day is, or ought to be, a great day for the ex-slaves. On that day, a quarter of a century ago, Lincoln issued his immortal Proclamation of Emancipation. I was told there would be service in their churches. I asked one negro after another where I should find the church in use. One guessed, another rather thought, a third believed, etc. They sent me hither and thither in their feckless way, but that church I never reached. I found our dark brothers on the quays, in the saloons, at their own doors, at the street corners, but nowhere at church. One impudent darkie sneeringly told me "I would make a lot of money at church." The almighty dollar had eaten into him too. After an hour's search in the rain I gave it up, and wandered instead to see the river, the cotton ships, and the levee. This latter, a huge bank of earth, is the guardian of the city. As the river has silted up the floods have risen higher, and the levee has had to be raised again and again, for the Mississippi now runs fifteen feet above the level of many of the streets. It would be easy to make an end of New Orleans.

In the afternoon I was lucky enough to meet young Mr. Watts, of the well-known London shipping firm of Watts, Ward & Co. Together we spent a pleasant evening, and at a reasonable hour I went to bed. One last sensation remained for me, however, before I turned in; one final proof, if such were needed, of the sensitive regard of the chivalrous Southerner for the feelings of a race. Amongst the printed list of warnings and instructions hung in the bedroom, I read in italics—*Beware of coloured washerwomen—theft and bugs.* When I paid my excessive bill in the morning, it was not of black men's theft I had need to complain. I discharged the account in silence, remembered my black brother who had assiduously attended to my comfort, crossed the river, took my seat on the cars, and left New Orleans without regret *en route* for the desert.

CHAPTER V.

AN EARTHLY PARADISE—THE WAY THITHER—DESERT—THE
MIRAGE—JUST IN MEXICO—CITIES OF THE WEST—THE
INDIAN IN PANTALOONS—LOS ANGELES—A MODEL HOME
—IRISHMEN IN THE WEST—LAND SPECULATION—ADVERTISING EXTRAORDINARY.

Hotel Nadeau, Los Angeles,
January 13th, 1889.

I HAVE apparently found a Paradise on earth. The road to it, like that to the Upper Paradise, is long and stony and tedious, but when you arrive the pain of striving is forgotten in the beatitude of possession. I left myself in New Orleans. The distance thence is 2000 miles, to cover which consumed three nights and four days in the cars. The country may be described in a sentence: 400 miles of swamp, 800 miles of a wilderness of trees and undergrowth interspersed with rude Texan clearings, 700 miles of horrible desert, and 100 miles of verdant beauty. Of Texas I have but space to repeat the witty description given by a bishop on the cars: "Texas has more rivers and less water, more cows and less butter, more creed and less religion, than any country." At one time we were 4500 feet above the sea, at another 200 feet below it. The desert must have been blood-curdling in pre-railway days. No water, no shelter, apparently no limit. Only sandy, rocky wastes with scarce a green thing on them, and no cover from the burning heat of the day or the tornadic winds and waterspouts which now and anon burst over them in fury. Now, however, thanks to George Stephenson, you career along as gaily as Apollyon's passengers in Hawthorne's Celestial Railroad, and when you reach the end, the desert,

HOMES IN LOS ANGELES.

TO THE GOLDEN LAND. 31

I repeat, is forgotten. Yet it was bad enough, and strange enough. Thrice in one day I saw in the far distance shining lakes of water, their banks lined with shadowy trees. Yet water there was not. It was but the mirage—wondrous sham; to us interesting merely, but to the pioneers and gold-seekers forty years ago how fatal a will-o'-the-wisp. I spoke just now of running along far below sea-level. It is even so. We crossed for eighty miles where once flowed the waters of the Californian Gulf. The very names of the stations tell of the terrors and escapes of a painful past: Sweet Water, Painted Rock, Mohawk Summit, Mammoth Tank, Flowing Well, Volcano Springs, Dry Camp, White Water. As in Sahara, the horrid distances are measured out by the names of the infrequent wells.

At El Paso I took advantage of a long delay to cross the Rio Grande and plant my feet in Mexico and in a Mexican town. The latter is commonplace and dirty. Yet it is grandiloquently termed a city. Indeed, there are cities everywhere *en route*. A few wooden dwellings are run up on unpaved streets, a wooden or brick court-house or town hall is reared, and forthwith you have a " city " in the Far West. Gila City consists of two wooden and two adobè, or dried clay, cabins; Yuma City is a bunch of shabby shanties *plus* a hotel, and so on. At Yuma I took my first look at the North American Indian in his native lair. Some thirty of the tribe, men and squaws, were at the station. Their long, thick, coal-black hair is their only head-covering. They affect the European costume, and the spectacle of the noble Red Man in a pair of patched shoddy pantaloons is ludicrous enough. These Yumas live and loaf at the expense of the American Government, and, as the guide-book hastens to assure nervous travellers, have never gone into the scalping business.

Yuma is on the banks of the great river Colorada, whose waters will by-and-by irrigate thousands of now arid square miles in Arizona and New Mexico. It is, I suppose, the sunniest place in the world, for 351 days per annum are sunny, and only fourteen cloudy. Crossing the

Colorada we are at last in California, though hours of desert-travelling still intervene between us and lovely Los Angeles. The first thing I did when at length we were fairly housed in that Elysium was—let me frankly confess it—to go to bed. In a journey of 2000 miles we were just fifteen minutes behind time.

The next day proved a day of brilliant sunshine, so that the capital of Southern California was presented to me under the most favourable conditions. It was the 6th of January, 1889; but with a blazing sun in a cloudless sky, the thermometer running up to 80, and a warm, balmy breeze playing on your cheeks, you might be pardoned for taking it to be the 6th of July. Los Angeles is situated in part on a level plain, about sixteen miles from the ocean and 200 feet above it, and in part on a succession of low hills to the north and west of the level land. A little river of the same name winds through the plain. Meek enough it looks now as I cross on its wooden bridge, but in the rainy season it is apt to become a boisterous and dangerous torrent. The city was colonised by the Spanish monks, who last century christianised California. They saw its beauty of situation, set themselves down there, and called it in their ornately-pious way the Town of the Queen of the Angels.

When the country passed to the United States in 1847, Los Angeles was a pretty village; in 1870 it had 4000 souls; in 1880, 11,000; now, in 1889, its imaginative citizens claim for it a population of 85,000, whilst even a cool on-looker cannot well place it at less than 60,000. Marvellous growth! How it comes to pass we may consider by-and-by. In the meantime let us saunter together and see what the Los Angeles of to-day is like. The two chief streets—Main and Spring Streets —are broad, level, and well-paved, parallel with one another for a long distance, and then merging into one avenue, which stretches away for miles in a straight line south. Tramcars occupy the centres. The broad sidewalks are flagged or cemented, and front rows of handsome shops, banks, hotels, etc., four and five storeys in

BOUNDARY STONE BETWEEN CALIFORNIA AND MEXICO.

height, reared in brick, freestone, or granite, and such architecturally as the streets of London would not be ashamed to possess. The newness of the town is evidenced by the fact that these gorgeous edifices are not continuous. Sandwiched in between them are the modest wooden shanties, the stores which served the first race of merchants and shopkeepers. Gradually these are being replaced, but enough remain to mark the rawness of the place. The other streets are yet unfinished, and sorely need the paving which is being pushed rapidly forward. In the prevailing dry weather they are wastes of dry dust, on the rare wet days seas of sticky mud. Pausing at this corner of Main Street you can grasp at a glance a fair idea of the city. Here is a towering block of handsome offices, there opposite a great red-brick hotel. Next to the former is a row of one-storeyed wooden shops, and as your eye shrinks from their rude ugliness it lights on a lovely ornamental private villa set back from the street. A row of feathery pepper-trees, laden with ruddy fruit, shades the sidewalk; a close-cut cypress hedge guards the trim lawn from the street; evergreens and orange-trees rich with yellow fruit attract the eye, and flowering shrubs tempt the smell; standard roses and tall lilies bloom in full luxuriance; geranium, canariensis, and white jasmine glorify the porch; whilst tall, stately gum-trees fill up the background of the picture. (Remember still this is the 6th of January.) Soon this lovely home must give place to shops; but hundreds such are scattered along the broad and stately avenues, which stretch out for miles in every direction from the Town of the Angels.

The streets are full of crowds of bustling men and bustled women. The silk hat of civilisation is absent; the soft felt, black or grey or white, teaches you that you are alike in the land of the democracy and the land of the Sun. The people are of every race under heaven—white and black and yellow and copper-coloured. Los Angeles is cosmopolitan. The hotel I stay at is owned by an Irishman; its manager is an American, the cook is a

German, a black brother waits on me, and a Chinaman washes my clothes. By the way, I am lucky in that hotel and its owner. So soon as my name was written on the register the proprietor sought me out, was kind enough to say he knew me by repute, and that he and all his staff were at my command to make my stay comfortable. He has more than kept his word. They are curious fellows these Irishmen, good lovers and good haters! I have met them everywhere over the State, and many of them in good positions too. Keenly interested in the old country, all of them. And it may, of course, be an accident, but it is the fact that I have only met one who is not a Nationalist.

Los Angeles may fairly be described as a busy city, the people shrewd, speculative, and, with due allowance for the enervating weather, industrious. It is the centre to which converge all the four great railway lines, whilst two more important ones are being driven on through it. Had it only possessed such a harbour as San Francisco, it might have rivalled that metropolis, for it is nearer to New York and the East. Unfortunately its so-called harbours, twenty or thirty miles off, are little better than open roadsteads. Indeed, San Diego, 135 miles south, is the only safe, commodious, and deep harbour in South California. Still Los Angeles will wax great. It is the centre of an immensely rich county, in which oranges, grapes, lemons, olives, walnuts, barley, and wheat grow luxuriantly, and who knows what the unexplored mountains round contain in mineral wealth? At the present time the city is not very prosperous. It is suffering from a cold fit after a fever. Last year they had what they call a landboom. Everybody speculated in land, bought plots or farms or sites, ran up the prices to ridiculous heights, the keen men getting out in time, the duller remaining, in the expressive phrase of the time—land-poor. They have plenty of land, but no dollars.

I call the city busy, but too many men are busy in the wrong way. They have the whole country round laid out in town sites till the population of a Liverpool or a

Glasgow might be accommodated here; only—Liverpools and Glasgows are not made in a year. They will have to learn that the true wealth of the country lies not in speculating in land but in digging the prolific soil, or in developing the mineral wealth of the mountains. Those things done, towns will come of themselves where they are needed, and not where speculators "rush" them. Meanwhile, the Los Angelians peg away, and build and scheme. At advertising dodges they whip the world. It is quite a diversion to wander through the streets and cull the odd conceits of enterprising tradesmen. One shoemaker announces, " The people's understandings renovated; ay, and their frail soles made whole;" a restaurant-keeper breaks into doggerel thus—

> " Handsome Dan,
> With his gang,
> Has sprang
> To 18 South Spring Street."

Whilst a third oddity magniloquently declares—" Pedal teguments artistically lubricated and illuminated for the infinitesimal compensation of ten cents per operation;" which, being interpreted into English, means—Shine your boots for fivepence.

In this Paradise they do not disdain the ways of earth.

CHAPTER VI.

A STRANGE LAND—DULL GEOGRAPHY—A GREAT BRITAIN AND A HALF—MEN WANTED—WHO SHALL COME—THE SOUTH—PASADENA AND THE RAYMOND—SPANISH SAINTS—DRAWBACKS IN THE LAND—SUMMER AND ITS STRANGENESS—VINEYARDS—LUCKY BALDWIN—HEALTH QUESTIONS—LAND AND ITS PRICES—CHINEE CHEAP LABOUR—BOYCOTTING EVEN IN CALIFORNIA.

Hotel Brewster, San Diego,
February 9th, 1889.

IF you care to follow me intelligently through California, I must perforce tell something of the country as a whole. Yet how to make matters clear to English people I know not, when one has to tell of a country carpeted with richest green in winter, brown as umber in summer; where the fruits ripen first in the north; where it is hot in the morning, cool at noon; where the hill-sides are warmer at night, cooler by day than the valleys; where umbrellas are useless in the rare drenching wet days, but potential mainly against the sun; where they go to the mountains for water, and dig in the valleys for roots for fuel; where they gather the orange crop in January, and take off seven crops of alfalfa (the Californian clover) in the season; where you wear thick clothing and underclothing in July as at Christmas; where it is bright and sunny 320 days in the year; where gold and silver fill the mountains and cattle cover the hills, and the golden orange and paler lemon and olives and figs and grapes the valleys; where oats and barley are grown for hay; where the roads are mended, and well mended, by being ploughed up; and where **guns** are called scatter-guns, pointers smell-dogs, and sportsmen proudly delight in " hunting " the jack-rabbit and the quail.

Yet of the land as a whole I must tell. So bear with me through some perchance dull description, geographical and otherwise. California, then, stretches for 600 miles along the Pacific between thirty-three and forty-two degrees North. San Francisco, its chief city, is in the latitude of Lisbon; San Diego, its southernmost city, in that of Alexandria. The country may be roughly described as lying between the Sierra Nevada Mountains and the ocean, though this is not strictly the fact, since it takes in not a few fertile valleys and much desert land on the eastern slopes of the range, beyond which desert the distant Rocky Mountains stretch north and south, the backbone of a continent.

The Sierra Nevadas, rough, craggy, frowning, rise to snow-capped peaks 11,000 feet high, and seem to bar, but bar in vain, the passage of the all-acquiring Anglo-Saxon to this Eden of the West. The State, one of forty in the mighty Republic, contains 181,000 square miles. It is therefore one and a half times the size of the whole British Isles, and its present population is one million and a quarter. Every temperature and every product of the soil is here. The hardy miner can dig wealth from the mountains; the physically-broken gain new health in the valleys. Of lawyers and clerks and speculators, and men who would fain live by their wits, there are enough and to spare; but agriculturists and gardeners and fruit-growers and men deft of hand can find here more than a living without all-absorbing toil. The climate won't let you kill yourself by drudging. Of two things let any who think of coming take note. You must have patience, for the soil, though prolific, will not yield its fruits in a night; and you must have a little money to look about you ere locating and to get along "till the kye come hame." These cautions given, believe me there is room here for two millions of working families; and that incubus of Europe, the landlord, need not rear here his ugly head, for the land can be bought at £5 or £10 an acre, and twenty or forty acres—according as it may be good or moderate—will suffice for a family's comfort. Do old-fashioned folk remember, perchance, Henry Russell's once-popular song (slightly modified)?—

> " To the West, to the West, to the land of the Free,
> Where fair California runs down to the sea;
> Where a man is a Man if he's willing to toil,
> And the humblest may gather the rich fruits of the soil.
>
> " Where children are blessings, and he who has most
> Has aid to his fortune and riches to boast;
> Where the young may exult and the aged may rest,
> Away, far away, in the land of the West."

There is the poetry of emigration; the prose of it is that you must rough it for a year or two, comforted by the thought that you are working for yourself, and not for another man.

It is, however, of Southern California that in this and a succeeding letter I wish to tell. At two-thirds of the distance from the northern frontier the Sierra Nevadas throw off a huge spur known as the San Bernardino Mountains, which stretch due west at a height of from 4000 to 11,000 feet till they reach the sea at Point Conception. These cut the State into two unequal portions. This Southern California—bounded on the north by the desert beyond the San Bernardino Range, on the east by the Sierra Nevadas, and on the west and south by the sea (for the Pacific runs sharply in here to the southeast)—contains, including Kern County, 58,000 square miles, and is therefore as large as England and Wales. Its present population is about equal to that of Dublin or Edinburgh, being under 300,000. Ample room and verge enough here for new men! Numerous smaller ranges of mountains intersect it in most admired disorder, leaving room for rich and spreading valleys through which flow the insignificant rivers, the lack of which in volume and number constitutes one of the landscapic defects of the country. O'er all the varied scene the sun seldom fails to shine in splendour, whilst a blue and smiling ocean kisses with pacific warmth the golden sands.

I have spent the last month scouring by rail, in buggy,

PASADENA.

or on foot, the hills and vales, the rising towns and the detached ranches of this favoured land, with Los Angeles, its capital, as my base of operations. It is not in the bustling capital you realise what the land is. Come with me to Pasadena, but eight miles away. Stand upon the rounded detached hill on which the Raymond Hotel raises its huge bulk, and gaze with delighted eye around. At your feet, nestling amid its orange groves, is Pasadena, a lovely town of villas and detached residences and hotels and shops, a residential offshoot of Los Angeles. On every side stretches the rich expanse of the San Gabriel Valley, the largest in Southern California. For ninety miles from west to east, and for twenty or thirty from north to south, it fills the eye, carpeted with green, its low hills adorned with live evergreen oaks, which set off the expanse of barley, wheat, and alfalfa, the orange groves, the vineyards, the orchards of apricot and peach, lemon and fig. Ever and anon darker patches indicate huge areas of scrub of wild sage and grease-wood covering the yet unbroken land. There on the left is the old San Gabriel Mission Church built by the Spanish Jesuits, who last century christianised the Indians, here a mild and gentle race. The wood was carried from the mountains on their patient backs, whilst, iron being unknown in the land, the rafters and slates were kept in place by strips of cow-hide.

The Jesuits are still on hand; here and there too are the scattered relics of their Indian converts: and if nothing else be left of the ancient Spanish domination, the names of the saints still survive to mark the towns and mountains and rivers. San Francisco, Santa Cruz, Santa Barbara, San Bernardino, Los Angeles, Santa Fe, San Diego, and a hundred other such names recall the rise and fall of the adventurous successors of Cortes and the band who transformed Mexico and its surrounding states into a New Spain.

But to our scene. White and dusty roads cross the valley in every direction, leading to and through thriving villages, and struggling settlements, and detached villas of delight; and a rough and stony expanse, sometimes a mile wide, marks where flows the San Gabriel River, now a scarcely-noticeable stream, but which from time to time vomits itself with desolating vigour over the vale. As frame-work to the picture the frowning mountains rise abruptly from the plain, crowned by snowy crests; best known among them is Old Baldy, as prominent a feature here as Snowdon or Schiehallion or the Jung-frau. The Pacific gleams in the west; a hot sun brightens the gay world; the ocean breeze comes softly up each day with noon; it is January; the thermometer registers 52 at 5 A.M., 50 at 5 P.M., 72 in the afternoon, 46 at night; it is delightful even to breathe; the atmosphere is so clear that the San Jacinto and San Gorgonio Mountains, ninety or a hundred miles away, seem close at hand. Does this seem a fairy sketch? Has poetic licence slaughtered truth? Are there no drawbacks? Yes; if you are lucky you may meet a brown bear in the mountains, or a stray rattlesnake in the cañons; the coyotes (the Californian wolf) howl round your home at nights, and make free with your chickens or maybe your lambs; the tarantula, the centipede, or the poison oak may sting you; or infrequent sand-storms blind you; whilst the roads on wet days are filled with liquid mud, in windy weather are thick with suffocating dust. But what of summer? Is it not excruciatingly hot? No; that is the wonder of it; or rather there are two wonders in summer. First of all, it is not much hotter than winter wherever the daily ocean breeze penetrates with its cooling and invigorating breath. Secondly, in July, August, September, and October, though the rivers are mostly dry, and rain never comes, and the green has changed to brown in the valleys and on the hill-sides, yet cattle and horses graze everywhere on the burnt-up vegetation, and thrive and *fatten*. The grasses and clovers have grown with a luxuriance unknown in England, and as mid-summer comes, are not cut and stacked as hay, but are allowed to dry down into hay standing on the land. The burr clover and the alfarilla develop a "burr" or berry full of essential oil, and with immense fattening properties. And there, I say, on burnt-up ranges whose appearance would fill the uninitiated with despair, the stock thrives. Water, too, is at hand. Though the rivers have left the surface, they run on underground five, ten, or twenty feet down, and everywhere little windmills, worked by the constant friendly breeze, dot the horizon, and give quaintness to the farmsteads. Elsewhere, irrigating channels convey the precious fluid from the mountains, whilst in yet other districts there is an ample artesian supply. In one way or another the early trouble as to water is being overcome. There need be no permanent difficulty in a country full of mighty ranges of snow-covered mountains.

So much for the scene from the terraced front of the Raymond Hotel. That hotel itself merits a passing notice. It is owned and managed by the same people who have the famous Crawford House in the White Mountains, just north of New York. There the season opens in June and closes in October; whereupon the entire hotel staff, running, I suppose, into hundreds, male and female, is put on board train, and transported 3000 miles across the continent, to open and work the Raymond from November till May. And admirably they do it. A pleasanter or more comfortable hotel even a grumbling John Bull could not desire. The Raymond season over, the locomotive whirls the Easterns back to resume another year's operations in New Hampshire. And so on year by year. A truly characteristic illustration of the magnificent American way of running hotels, each containing accommodation for hundreds of guests.

On one of our pleasant drives we visited two of the great vineyards and wineries of the valley. The Sunnyside Winery, owned by an English company, for which I understand Sir John Puleston, M.P., negotiated the purchase at the price of 1,000,000 dollars, had 400,000 gallons in stock, and the adjoining Baldwin Winery no less than 500,000. We had a "tasting" afternoon at clarets, burgundies, hocks, sherries, and ports, all of course for our improvement in knowledge. I feel bound to say that, with the single exception of some fifteen-year-old port, there was no wine likely to attract Englishmen's palates.

The career of the owner of this latter property is a typical Californian one. He is popularly known as Lucky Baldwin, and began his career as keeper of a saloon and restaurant in San Francisco. With his savings he bought stock in the new Pacific Railroad, and, taking the scrip with him, went off for a prolonged tour in China and Japan. When he returned he found this scrip enormously increased in value and himself rich. Judicious investment followed. Amongst other possessions he acquired this ranch of 55,000 acres. The purchase money was of trivial amount, yet if he chose to break up the estate now he could probably sell it for a million sterling. He spends his time in breeding and running race-horses, and is seldom here, preferring the delights of San Francisco to the quiet pleasures of his country home. Lucky Baldwin! California has done well for him. What good things he does or means to do for California I know not.

Some of my readers, yearning to find health or fortune, may pardon—nay, perhaps thank me—if I forestall their inquiries at this point. First, as to health. This is a land of promise for those threatened with, or suffering from, consumption, asthma, throat diseases, dyspepsia, or physical prostration. There is no enervating heat in summer, no paralysing cold in winter, no snow save on the mountains, no frost worth mentioning, no continuous damp and foggy weather. The air is pure and inspiring; it is possible to live much in the open air, to keep your windows open all night and day, to sleep in tents if you please, for months together. What this means for those inclined to consumption, doctors know. Infectious diseases are scarcely known, the death-rate is extremely low, and life indeed worth living. To secure these advantages, however, you must not choose Los Angeles or the lands near the sea, and still less the bottom valley lands, for there the chill and the frost gather in the nights. Get on the hill-sides. My friend Mr. J. G. Blumer, so well known in the North, and with whom I have been happy to renew a pleasant acquaintance, lives, to his manifest physical advantage, 1200 feet up on a charming hill-side at Sierra Madre, with the mountains behind him and the light fog of the valley below him. Another friend who came here three years ago ill is regaining his old form at 800 feet up. A third, with whom we start for a tour in three days, arrived fourteen years ago to die. California has made him ruddy and strong. Five hundred feet up or more—that is his advice. I refrain from saying more, lest a shipload of invalids arrive ere I depart. Suffice it to add that when once full knowledge of this incomparable land has reached our European physicians, it is not to Algiers or Madeira or Canary that they will send their patients as a last chance.

Now, to those who dream of finding fortune here what shall I say? Why, that Fortune is fickle. But if it is a sufficiency you want, and fair returns for labour and capital, Southern California will give you these, and this under physical conditions of ease and comfort which may fairly be counted as part of your wage. You can buy good unimproved land with water for £10 or £12 an acre. If you extend the payment over a series of years you must be prepared to pay 8 per cent., for money is scarce and dear here. The country is rich as yet only in natural resources. Land less good can be had as low as at £6 or £7 per acre; good improved land, planted out in vines, oranges, or apricots, at from £40 to £75 per acre. Upon twenty or thirty acres of the latter a family can make a comfortable living, save, and have the amplest leisure. Of unimproved land it will be well to have 60 or 100 acres for comfort. Drudging, continuous toil is not needed; the necessities don't require it, the climate won't allow it. Ladies must be prepared to do much that they can get servants to do in England. For here help is scarce. Your Californian loves to be his own master. If he works for you his wages eat up much of the profit, and the inevitable effect of this is to prevent the aggregation of estates and divide the land among the many; which is well. I know of six young ladies who came out from the Eastern States to be school teachers. Finding no opening, they, with true American adaptability, applied for waiters' places at one of the new big hotels. Each has her own bedroom; they have a sitting-room, with piano, their food, and £60 a year a-piece. Only the Chinese, who are here in thousands, stand between many a family and discomfort, and enable the thrifty to get their land tilled where the labour of the family itself does not suffice.

The Chinese question is a burning one. The laws prohibit further immigration; many favour the expulsion of those already here; leagues are being formed to boycott those who employ them, and the papers daily teem with letters of denunciation. One such merits mention for its sublime impudence. The writer denounces the Chinese, and declares that, willing to work, he has been forced into idleness by cheap competition till, driven to desperation, he has committed theft, and now (poor ill-used fellow) writes from the interior of a gaol! We attended one meeting at Riverside (that loveliest home of the orange) to form such a league there. Whilst the orators were thundering in favour of substituting for "cheap inferior Chinese labour" "good honest reliable white labour"—such are the cant phrases—the shock of a slight earthquake startled the land. Evidently the gods are against John Chinaman. But for my part I do not see how the rough work of clearing off the scrub is to be economically achieved without him, and I know many a lady between whom and drudging discomfort stand as her only defence her Chinese male cook and her Chinese male washerwoman. But let the Mongol question rest.

The practical moral of the above is this: if you or your family need a perfect clime to secure or regain your health, and *if you have some money*, Southern California is the ideal land for you.

> " All nature seems in unison complete,
>   And scarce a sound or welcome wind that blows
> But speaks of happiness, and life replete
>   With all conditions that contentment knows."

And the tea it is come
from the Chinese country
Some tea growing in the
field and Some growing the
mountains in the Spring time
they are grown-up And the
Summer time and the farmer
go and cut them down and
take out which young
one and which old one and
put out the Sun And dry
up And the young one call
a good tea and the old
one call not very good

Who Shall ascend into the
hill of the Lord or who
Shall stand in his holy place

ESSAY BY A CHINESE COOK AT SCHOOL.

CHAPTER VII.

ODDS AND ENDS—GLADSTONE EVEN HERE—OFF TO RIVERSIDE—PROHIBITION CITIES—A SUNDAY MORNING SCENE—SOMETHING FOR THE CHILDREN—SAN DIEGO, THE CITY OF THE BAY—A PRESENT NAPLES; A FUTURE LIVERPOOL—CLIMATE PAST COMPARE—A LOW DEATH-RATE—THE GREAT HOTEL—AN AMERICAN DIVES AND HIS CAR.

Hotel Brewster, San Diego,
February 20th, 1889.

FROM the Los Angeles district I have passed to San Diego and its county, accompanied by two most pleasant Americans, one a valued friend of seven years' standing. It was with regret I left that lovely San Gabriel Valley; still more do I regret (though my readers may not share this feeling) that I have not space to enter more largely into detailed description of the many new and interesting things and scenes we saw there. I should have liked to describe a visit to the nearest seaside resort of the Los Angelians, Santa Monica, where I was most pleasantly entertained by Mr. and Mrs. Walter Wren, the son-in-law and daughter of Mr. Richard Sheraton; and to the Soldiers' Home which is being erected there by the U.S. Government for 4000 or 5000 of the veterans of the Great War, and is but one of several now rising in various parts of the country. What is to be done with these palatial homes when the veterans shortly die off I know not, nor could the gallant colonel in charge enlighten me. They may be transformed into workhouses or hospitals; more probably they will remain as monumental proofs of the building folly of a too-rich Government which does not quite know how to get rid of its tremendous surpluses. I should like to have been able to tell, too, of the Arrowhead Hot Springs and Mud Baths, a charming resort in the mountains, destined at some not-distant day to be as famous as Pfeffers; a drive up one of the canons, which wind sometimes for miles deviously into the mountains; and of a stroll into the rocky wilderness which forms in dry times the bed of the San Gabriel river, and where, when oppressed by the mid-day sun, I came upon a huge solitary boulder, whereon was inscribed in fair square letters the magic name Gladstone. Incontinently I sat upon Gladstone and smoked a cigarette in honour of the Grand Old Man. Just let me interpolate here a fact vouched for by my friend Mr. Blumer. He happened to attend one of the recent election meetings at Los Angeles. There was much cheering of well-known men and names, but the loudest cheers of all were elicited by a passing reference to the veteran statesman who stands for Californians as the typical Englishman. Salisbury and all the other marquises and dukes piled together don't bulk so large in their eye as the single Liberal chief who has three times ruled the British Empire, and may probably rule it again.

It might much amuse, too, if I made my readers acquainted with strange, unlooked-for personages, cast by the ocean of circumstance upon these cosmopolitan shores; with the sons of John Brown, of Harper's Ferry fame, settled here in their mountain-home; with the nephew of an English bishop, who at one not-distant period of his chequered career turned an honest penny by taking the ten-cent pieces at the door of a dime-show; with the nephew of Garibaldi running a saloon; the son of a most famous Confederate General selling land and houses on commission; or the nephew of Washington Irving cultivating his ranch and happy with his Indian squaw. The motto of California is, or ought to be—Get along anyhow and anywhere, but get along. My motto now must be—Forbear.

The direct road to San Diego is by the coast-line railway, the distance south from Los Angeles being 135 miles. We preferred to take the longer and more

picturesque route (180 miles long inland through the mountains, resting for a couple of days in the Riverside region. The history of Riverside is fairly illustrative of the history of multitudes of Californian places. It used to be accounted part of the arid, waterless Californian desert. Keen-eyed men passed that way; they saw that the so-called waste was covered with deep rich soil whitened by the sun; they acquired the land, diverted part of the waters of the Santa Anna river, carried two irrigating streams through their possessions, and now you see a pretty town full of detached dwellings, surrounded by orange groves rich these February days with their golden fruit, and ride along a magnificent avenue seven miles long by 100 feet wide, and shaded by spreading magnolia and eucalyptus trees, through which may be seen the picturesque homes of a comfortable people.

Riverside presents one aspect doubtless of deep interest to many English persons. It is a prohibition town; nor does it stand alone in its glory, for I have been also at Duarte, Escondido, San Marcos, Elsinore, and other townsteads, all places where no saloons are permitted, where even the hotels have to be teetotal, and where the only *modus operandi* of getting liquor (if you don't carry a sly supply) is to get a doctor's certificate of weak health, and then supply yourself from the drug-store! In some cases the system flows from the initiative of the inhabitants; in others, from the will of the landowners, whose deeds of transfer of plots contain a clause prohibiting all liquor-shops. These prohibition communities all have their public halls and numerous churches belonging to various denominations, whilst the peace officers have about as much to do as the extraordinary Spanish policeman whom I found last year at Orotava, in Teneriffe, and who used, in despair of finding other delinquents, to get drunk himself every Sunday evening, so as to keep the magistrates in practice once in the week, on the Monday morning.

A propos of the churches, I recall one Sunday morning scene in front of a hotel I was staying at. Before meeting-time a row of omnibuses drew up on the terrace, whilst the bustling conductors called out—" Presbyterians this way; Episcopalians here; Methodists in the blue 'bus; Unitarians along here; Congregationalists this way." And the gaily-dressed crowd filed off and went smilingly each to worship God after his own lights, no man regarding his brother as a heretic. This in a land which, according to the cant phrase of our British Establishment-men, dishonours and disowns God by not having a State Church! Is there no true religion here? Does God, one wonders, look with less delight on such a scene than on a land where one portion of His children looks on another as heretics and schismatics? There are numerous handsome schools, too, full of healthy, bright boys and girls, one of the latter of whom (I print this sweet folly because I cannot forget to amuse the children) it must have been who was responsible for the following essay :—

"THIS IS A COW.

"A cow is an animal with four legs on the under side. The tail is longer than the legs, but is not used to stand on. The cow kills flies with its tail. A cow has big years that wiggles on hinges; so does their tail. The cow is bigger than the calf, but not so big as an elephant. She is made so small that she can go in the barn when nobody is looking. Some cows are black, and some hook. A dog was hooked once. She tossed the dog that worried the cat that killed the rat. Black cows give white milk; so do other cows. Milkmen sell milk to buy their little girls dresses, which they put in water and chalk. Cows chew cuds, and each finds its own chew. That is all there is about cows."

Ignoring the earthquake, which we afterwards heard of, but did not at the time feel, we proceeded from Riverside south by Lake Elsinore, through the Temecula Canon, a narrow defile as wild, if not as historically romantic, as Glencoe, past the enormous Margharita Ranch of 208,000 acres, on which feed 30,000 cattle, and so to Oceanside, and along the sea coast to San Diego.

This city is destined to be one of the great ports of the world. With an area half as large again as Great Britain, California has only a sea coast of some 700

ORANGE GROVES.

miles, and on it but two really good harbours—San Francisco to the north, and San Diego to the south, with nearly 500 miles between them. Both are landlocked harbours of great size. At San Diego a large semi-circular bay, much like an inverted ↄ, runs in, the rocky headlands at its extremities being perhaps twenty miles apart. Half-way down the bay a narrow low-lying flat tongue of land shoots out to the north like a shovel-handle, widening out at its top like the shovel, and leaving only a passage of a few hundred yards between it and the sheltering northern highland, Point Loma. On the bar there is a depth of twenty-three feet at low water, twenty-eight feet at high; ships can enter and leave with perfect ease and safety in all weathers; inside there is a bay twelve miles long by from one to two broad, perfectly sheltered, absolutely safe, containing nearly three square miles of area twenty-four feet deep, and nearly one and a half square miles thirty-six feet. Here is a harbour the Lord hath made. It is the natural door of Southern California—a country, let me repeat, as large as England. Imagine England with one such harbour, and one only. Think what that harbour and its town would be; and then do not doubt as to the mighty future of San Diego; which does not, however, pin all its fortunes to California solely. Behind the mountains lie Arizona and other regions, by-and-by to be filled with people, and all wanting a safe outlet to the western sea. Nor is all said yet. San Diego is 400 miles nearer to New York than San Francisco is, and the railroads thither pass over much lower passes and through more genial climes than the northern snow-threatened routes. It is, moreover, 500 miles nearer to Australia and New Zealand than its sister port. By San Diego in consequence the mails must soon come, for to save two days means so much. Still more remains. When the Panama and the Nicaraguan Canal (one or both) are finished, as they will be, California, now 11,000 miles by sea from New York and 14,000 from London, will be distant but 4000 and 7000 miles respectively. San Diego being to the south 500 miles from San Francisco will be so much the nearer to Europe and the Eastern States, and will attract to itself much of the increasing traffic. It will export the corn, the olive oil, the wine, the cattle, the ripe and dried fruits, the silver and gold of the west, and gather in return tributes of produce from every land across the seas, despite a paralysing tariff. My life on't, San Diego will be the Liverpool of the Pacific, and when it is San Diegans will be for Free Trade. Such a port is worthy of the notice of our enterprising British merchants and shipowners. It imports its coals mainly from Australia, and coal sells by retail at 50s. per ton. Its cement —now largely used, and to be used still more largely in the future—comes from England, for none can be made in the States for lack of material, and cement retails at 70s. to 74s. per English ton. Here are margins. More than one English firm has already trading connections here, and as return cargoes become more certain and varied the number will assuredly increase.

To justify one's forecast of the future the city must have shown signs of rapid progress in the past. Note these facts. The population of San Diego in 1850 was 650; in 1875, 2500; in 1888, 32,000. It is laid out on a plan in broad streets at right angles, covering the flat land on the east of the bay and the rising ground beyond; the main streets are being rapidly paved; the whole city is admirably sewered with thirty-eight miles of glaced terra-cotta pipes, the surface water flowing separately from the sewerage; there are excellent tramcar and telephone services; the streets are lighted by gas and the electric light; an ample supply of drinking water has been brought from the Cuyamaca Mountains, fifty miles away, by an aqueduct or flume, partly of red-wood open casing and partly of iron pipe; the city is the proud possessor of a park of 1400 acres, from which the views of mountain and ocean are entrancing; and in the bay wharves enable the largest vessels to load and unload without lighterage, the railway cars running alongside the ships. Surely there is enough in the above to tell of an energetic, enterprising,

ORANGE PACKING.

and self-reliant community, governed by municipal and health authorities with heads on their shoulders.

But Nature too has showered her blessing on the city of the bay. The climate is superb. From an interesting work, the able and intelligent author of which I have had the pleasure of meeting often, I gather the following striking and authenticated statistics:—During the ten years 1876-1885, embracing 3653 days, there were 3533 on which the mercury never rose above 80 in the shade, and only twenty-seven in which it went above 90. During the same ten years there were 3560 days when the glass never fell below 40, and only two when it fell to 32. San Diego, therefore, like a Laodicean, is neither hot nor cold, but will scarcely be condemned to the Laodicean's fate. It is pleasantly warm by day, pleasantly cool by night. The average number of clear days for fifteen years is 184; of fair days, 136; of cloudy, forty-five; total, 365. The average number of days on which rain fell was thirty-four. It is only fair to add that when it does rain here it comes down with true American dash. Every drop is a dollar.

It is not to be wondered at that with such gracious gifts from Nature, and with enlightened sanitary management, infectious disease should be rare and the death-rate remarkably small. In the month of December it was at the rate of 4.5 per 1000 per annum; for the six months then ending it was at the rate of 7.5 per 1000 per annum! And this, although weak, broken-down Eastern and British people come here to recover or die.

It is from University Heights, rising 450 feet above the bay, that you realise how beautiful San Diego is. Mount the heights with me this gay, bright, smiling, hot February morning; or if you be indolent, the electric motor shall take you up. Now gaze around. Has earth a scene more fair? At your feet are the quaintly-varied buildings which constitute the as yet uncompleted city; beyond it is the bay glistening in the sun and just stirred into rustling motion by the welcome daily ocean breeze; then your eye takes in the low expanse of Coronada Beach, whose newly-planted avenues and groves give promise of early luxuriance, and on which towers the very largest, and I think in its architecture the most quaintly beautiful, hotel in the whole world; the waters of the blue Pacific wash its terraces, and stretch away far beyond where the rocky outlines of the Coronada Islands cut the sky. Point Loma, with its lighthouse, guards the bay; and False Bay, where the Jesuit fathers first landed, fills in the picture to the north. Southward, twenty miles away, rise, tier on tier, the mountains of Mexico, whilst to the east ranges of rolling uplands and green swelling hills lead the eye to rugged peaks, above which rise the snow-capped tops of Cuyamaca and the Volcan. A wondrous scene of tranquil beauty. Were San Diego rich with the historic and romantic associations which render Naples so entrancing, I know not to which bay of beauty I should give the palm.

During my rather prolonged stay at the City of the Bay I made my home on the mainland, spending, however, a few days at the great Coronada Beach Hotel, with its 750 rooms, its dining-hall, where 1000 guests can be seated, its ball-room, where 300 couples can together adorn the floor. The surf of the Pacific sings your lullaby, and the sun over Cuyamaca is your awakener. Every visitor should see this mighty caravansary, but the inconvenience of the ferry across the bay deters many from making it their home. It was here I met my first specimen of Dives travelling in his own railway-car. Your rich American who wants to cut a figure does not build a castle or a yacht; he gets to himself a luxurious, shiny car, with drawing-room, dining-room, bath-room, plush seats, silk curtains, hot water taps, and heaven knows what. At each town where he rests he takes good care that the local newspaper shall describe his magnificence; when he goes out "hunting" quail a paragraph informs a wondering world that "the thrice-millionaire" has bagged three brace; at each hotel he honours every one must make way for the man with the car. The particular individual who projected himself into the Coronada (a very decent fellow probably

HOTEL DEL CORONADA.

if his countrymen did not fool him so) appropriated the table and the waiter which had suited me for several days. Could a true-born Briton submit to this? Complaint at the office gave no relief against the man with the car. I examined the visitors' book and found the following entry—

> Jones Montmorency Steers and valet.
> Mrs. Jones Montmorency Steers and maid.
> Master Jones Montmorency Steers and governess.

Montmorency, thought I to myself, is a good name when you own it, but in this conjunction it reminds one of Jacob's description of his son Issachar—a strong ass crouching between two burdens. It was too much. I packed my bag, left the magnifico and the waiter to their enjoyment of one another, and transferred myself to the Brewster, where you have solid comfort, and where they know the value of a downright grumbling John Bull.

CHAPTER VIII.

SAN DIEGO AND ITS BACK-COUNTRY—A USEFUL CHAMBER OF COMMERCE—A TRIP TO THE MOUNTAINS—DUTCHMEN TO THE FRONT—LOVELY EL CAJON—WATER SCHEMES—A SAIL BETWEEN SKY AND EARTH—CHINAMEN AND INDIANS—IN THE MOUNTAINS AT LAST—THE HIDDEN VALLEY—A CALIFORNIAN WEDDING—A MOUNTAIN SETTLEMENT—FALLBROOK—NOT EVEN A CORKSCREW ON PRINCIPLE—AN ALPINE SCENE IN THE LAND OF THE SUN.

San Diego, March 1st, 1889.

WHEN at Los Angeles we announced our intention of exploring San Diego County, we were told we should find an enterprising city, a fine bay, a charming climate, but beyond that—nothing. That is the theory of the Los Angelians about their southern competitor. They tell you there is no back-country, little agricultural land, nothing to feed the town. English-like, we resolved to see for ourselves whether this could be true of a country of 14,000 square miles—*i.e.*, twice the size of the Principality of Wales. Six weeks sufficed to convince us that the theory is absolutely belied by the facts. Our resolve was whetted by a visit we paid, under the guidance of the active British Vice-Consul, Colonel Allen, to the San Diegan Chamber of Commerce. That body is happy in the possession of Mr. Turrell, a gem of a secretary, in whose enterprising hands no idea for making widely known the resources and capabilities of the country is allowed to lie fallow. In the rooms of the Chamber is a remarkable display of mineral and vegetable products. One saw there potatoes twenty inches round, cauliflowers eighteen inches across, pumpkins four feet long, maize fifteen feet high, vine shoots of forty-five feet, and a perfectly

bewildering display of oranges, lemons, apples, pears, raisins, prunes, apricots, peaches, and all kinds of vegetables; cotton, honey, wheat, and barley; granite and sandstone, lime as white as driven snow, magnetic iron ore, gold and silver-bearing quartz; sections of live oak, pine, and sycamore. And so on. Whence came the products? We determined absolutely to see this wondrous "back-country," if it existed.

Fortune made us acquainted with Mr. T. S. Vandyke, an East-country lawyer, who came here twelve or fourteen years ago, as the doctors thought, to die. He chose a pleasant home at Fallbrook, spent three years in roaming the hills and shooting deer, and stands now a living proof of what Southern California can do for those whom consumption apparently has doomed. No one knows the back-country so well as he; and his book, *Southern California*, written out of fulness of knowledge, and in strong, nervous English, is rightly regarded as a work of authority. To him it was proposed that he should join our band, and he fell in with our views. Behold us, then, a party of five (for my son had run across from Australia to spend his twenty-first birthday with me), two of Dutch extraction, three of English, ready to set out; our conveyance, a four-wheeled waggon without top or sides (nothing of that sort is needed here), set on strong springs, provided with a stout pole, and drawn by a couple of tough and wiry horses, which, let me interpolate, we returned to their stable at the end of the tour as fresh and plump as when they set out. So strong were they, so kind were we.

It was a sunny morn. Our way lay due east up towards the mountains, over rolling hills and tableland. Here and there were signs of the plough, whilst rough wooden dwellings proclaimed the recent advent of settlers. But as a rule these rolling uplands, untouched by man's toil, were only covered with scrub of grease-wood and wild sage, whose size and luxuriance proclaimed the wasted virtues of the virgin soil. We saw many a time thickets of scrub nine to ten feet high. For two hours we jolted along over a too-much-used road, rising gradually till, just beyond Dan Manning's Half-way House (Dan is an honest Irishman out from Youghal these forty years, and looks much more like a country squire than an Irish peasant, whilst his Californian home is pleasant to see), we were 700 feet above the sea; and suddenly the land fell away before us, and there below was the Valley of El Cajon (Spanish for The Box), a flat and spreading plain, lately a sheep-ranch, but now full of pleasant homesteads, and green with barley or planted out in vineyards and orchards. It was the first of the internal valleys, girt on every side with hills, to meet our eyes; and truly the sun had never seemed to us to shine upon a scene more fair than this unexpected oasis amongst the hilly wastes. For here was the surprise of it. Looking east when we started we could see fifty miles away the snow-capped mountains, whilst between the city and them rose tier on tier of gaunt and rocky points and swells, suggestive it might be of grandeur, but not of quiet, fruitful beauty. And lo! here, nestled amongst the wilds, lay sweet El Cajon with its forty square miles of fertile plain, not counting its rolling hill-sides, once thought valueless, but now by the discerning ploughed to the top for barley or planted with orange, apricot, and vine. Nor was El Cajon alone. It proved but the precursor to us of many broad and rich and lovely valleys scattered among the mountains, and gradually being brought under the fruitful yoke of industrious man.

Dropping down into the valley just where the flume leaves and the new Cuyamaca railroad enters it, we drove for an hour and a half across the plain, rounded some low hills, skirted the banks of the San Diego river, and, as the sun sank in the west and the chill of the February evening fell on the valley, the Lakeside Hotel appeared in view, and opened to us its welcoming doors.

There is one remarkable feature in El Cajon, the work not of nature but of man, and of which notice may best be taken here. For miles along the hill-sides runs the "flume" to which I referred above. Britons, accustomed

THE GREAT FLUME

to a copious rainfall, may well ask—what is a flume, and what its use? Well, it is an aqueduct constructed of red pine, a wood proved to be admirably adapted for this purpose, since in the north of California there exist such water-ways sound and good after the wear and tear of forty years. San Diego City has but an average rainfall of nine inches; the rolling country above it to the height of 500 or 600 feet has only eighteen inches; the higher lands, up to 2000 feet, double this rainfall again; whilst amidst the highest mountains even sixty inches fall. Now, for the rising cities on the coast, and for the contiguous mesas or tablelands, some hundreds of feet high and probably half a million acres in extent, water is the prime necessity. Without it these mesas are of little value; with it they are to be preferred to the valleys. For to these latter, when the sun sets, the cold air falls, and the frost comes in winter; whereas the mesas are warm and frostless by night, whilst the cool daily ocean breeze tempers the heat of the mid-day sun. Had I to choose, I would sooner, both for health and wealth's sake, have forty acres of watered mesa or hill-side than eighty acres in the loveliest of valleys.

Water is king in Southern California. They who bring it to the aid of the settler, while doubling the extent of arable land, will make every existing acre more productive, and, if no public statue be raised in honour of them, they will earn what most Americans prize more highly—plenty of dollars.

It may be thought that the numerous rivers can be readily utilised. But the rivers of Southern California are a most unsatisfactory race; as one paradoxical fellow put it, their bottoms are on top. They rise amidst the high mountains, and for the first half of their course force their turbulent way down rocky ravines and dreary chasms, till at thirty miles or so inland they reach one of the deep valleys which stretch in from the sea, and which at this distance are perchance only 200 or 300 feet above it. Along those valleys, over deep and shifting sands, they drivel along till the sands lick them up; they disappear;

miles from the ocean only dry and sandy wastes remain to mark their beds. Once in a way, when the infrequent rainstorms come, they pour down resistless floods to the sea, but soon shrink away underground again as though ashamed of such sportive energy in a land sacred to indolence.

If the rivers are to be subdued, you must assail them in the mountains. The bold projectors of the Great Flume have diverted the course of the San Diego river high up in the Cuyamaca Mountains, created there a huge reservoir or lake, and then carried their pine aqueduct for thirty-five miles along the sides of mountains, through tunnels, across valleys on giddy bridges. The water-way is four feet in breadth and (is to be) four feet high. At the foot of El Cajon the woodwork ends, the water being thence conveyed in iron pipes to reservoirs above the city, and so into it. San Diego has therefore an ample supply of excellent mountain water. But this is not all. All the way along the route the water is being, or will be, used for cultivation; which means in good years increased fertility, and might in dry years involve salvation of the crops. This great and beneficent work is said to have cost under one million dollars.

One of the pleasantest and oddest trips I ever made was over the surface of this flume. I expressed a wish to make this trip, and the obliging manager at Lakeside had a boat taken up the mountain on a waggon. It was a long narrow craft, drawing six or eight inches only, and provided with comfortable chairs, on which a party of six (two of them ladies) took their places, and away we went. The flume, as I said, is only four feet wide. It is meant also to be four feet deep, but at present only one board of fifteen inches forms its side, and we had but nine or ten inches of water to float us on. It was marvellous to glide in silence along the green mountain sides, a cloudless sky above us, the beauteous valleys below, and the soft, cool ocean breeze fanning our cheeks. Anon we disappeared into a tunnel. It took us twenty-three minutes to pass through the longest of these, and to add to our pleasure we stuck in the middle, and one of the party (not I) had to jump in

VIADUCT ON THE FLUME.

and pull us over the slight obstruction. Then out into the sunlight again, and away over the wooden aqueduct at a dizzy height across a valley. A hundred and fifty feet below us the cattle were grazing, whilst the startled quail scurried among the scrub, ground squirrels and gophers peeped out at the strange disturbers of their safe retreats, and the larks sang melodious in the morning air. This gopher, half a squirrel, half a mole, is a nuisance in the land. He burrows into the rich deep soil, his nimble paws fill a pouch with which he is provided round his neck, and then he comes above and deposits his load. Cultivation will slay him, but meanwhile horsemen, even on the roads and still more on the greensward, have to be wary, or they may meet the fate of the late Bishop Wilberforce—a broken neck.

At one o'clock we tied up our boat and lunched on the mountain. Remember still, remember ever, it was February. We basked in the sun, gathered the yellow violet, the yellower Californian poppy, shooting-stars and white forget-me-nots, and thought of the dear ones at home. Ah, lovely land! Ah, hours of peace and bliss! All the afternoon we glided down, and then the waggon met us and whisked us off to the hotel. *En route*, in a charming glen, we came upon a Chinese encampment. The Celestials had been busy clearing out the scrub, and now, their daily labour done, were resting under the shadow of the oaks. One was cooking, another washing clothes, three were playing at cards. I doubt not it was euchre, and Bill Nye wasn't there!

Nearer the hotel we passed a couple of Indians mounted on their unkempt mustangs. A wild pair, dressed in shabby civilised attire, their heads crowned with the everlasting wide-awake. They carried no fire-arms, only bows and arrows of the most primitive type. We examined the latter with much curiosity. They are made of a light wood; into the end a hole is drilled or burnt, and points of harder wood are inserted. With such insufficient arms of offence, the meek Christianised redman follows the chase, not unsuccessfully either. If his arrows fail, he will follow the great jack-rabbits, as big as and swifter than our hares, at breakneck speed along steep hill-sides, and bring them down with short, stout clubs, which he throws with unerring skill. It was odd to watch these Indians enter the store and buy their supplies like your even Christian. Their arithmetic not being equal to casting up a total, they priced, bought, and paid for each article in turn, got the change, and then proceeded to the next. We watched them ride tranquilly away, and then turned our faces to the hotel. As we reached it the evening sun was sinking behind the western hills. His last rays fell on the peaceful lake, where the wild ducks and water-hens were gathering, and lit up with pink radiance the mighty form of El Cajon Peak. How that peak reminds one of Honister Crag! A brief space, and the sun was gone, and darkness fell upon the scene.

We lingered several days in this lovely retreat, exploring the valleys and canons, amongst which the palm must be given to the glen El Monte, down which the San Diego glides, and whose rich greensward, shaded by umbrageous live-oaks, would make the sweetest picnic ground in the world. Lakeside and El Monte will be the choice country resort of the San Diegans, for on the 20th of this month the railroad will be opened, and the iron horse will convey the wise to the peaceful hill-sides. At last we tore ourselves away, forded the river, and headed for the further mountains. A day's journey up the passes brought us in view of Santa Maria, another great valley, 1500 feet above the sea, as large as El Cajon, not so rich and beautiful, but consisting of excellent wheat and barley land, and presenting a delightful view of the snow-tipped Volcan and the mightier Cuyamaca Peak. We spent the night in a quaint, comfortable hotel at Ramona, our bedrooms opening direct into an outside, sunny verandah. The February night was warm and pleasant; we needed no more covering than in England in June. Next morning we utilised in a trip to the Pamo Valley, a depression perhaps three miles long, shut in at every point, save one narrow gorge, by noble hills, and through which the Santa Ysabel or Barnardo

TUNNEL IN THE FLUME.

river makes its way. Some day soon, depend upon it, this Pamo Valley will be the bed of a huge and easily-constructed artificial lake, whence streams of fertility will be poured on the yearning land. On this trip the sportsman of our party (who shall be nameless) had the first shot with his Winchester rifle at Californian game in the person of a great jack-rabbit, and brought him down in style. Do not laugh at the jack-rabbit as game; or ere you do, turn your best English greyhounds on him, and he will laugh at them and you. Hereabouts they are not numerous, but further north are most destructive to the growing grain. If the rabbit has proved too much for the Australians, the Californians are too much for his bigger brother. Ever and again a whole country side gathers on horseback, scours the district, and drives thousands of jack-rabbits before it into a huge staked corral, ready prepared, wide at the neck and narrowing inwards, where the terrified animals are knocked on the head. At one of these *battues* 7000 bit the dust. See the sketch of one where 2500 lie in grim, picturesque silence. Is it cruel? No; it is expedient that they die so that man may live.

Returning from lunch to Ramona, we headed north-west, and made our way through rich tablelands and lonely gorges and noble passes. At 4 P.M. we rested on some rocks, where 1000 feet below lay, sun-steeped, the rich and verdant vale of San Pasqual. A breakneck run down the mountain brought us thither. We crossed the Barnardo river, mounted the opposing hills, passed a gold mine, and as night fell reached Escondido. Escondido! The Hidden! It should have been the name for the whole country. Here we found a prosperous and growing settlement with a handsome college of the Methodist Episcopal Church, a charming hotel, a jovial host, and a Chinese cook who ought to be made a mandarin. Escondido is a Prohibition district, as are San Marcos and Fallbrook. No liquor there—except on the sly.

Next morning we diversified our proceedings by assisting at a Californian wedding, where the loveliest girl I have seen these twenty years was married by the Catholic priest. After the breakfast the father of the bride accompanied us on a run to Bear Valley. We climbed a heavy mountain grade for miles, apparently into rocky wastes, and there burst upon our astonished gaze mountain-valley after mountain-valley green with grain. It was marvellous. Still more so was it to learn that 1000 feet above us still, on the top of the great mountain Palomares, was another prosperous settlement boasting a school-house and an election precinct. Palomares cast forty votes at the recent election. Its climate up there in the sky is better than that of England; its soil more rich, its products more profuse and varied. We returned by another route, down which all but the driver had to walk. On the hill-sides it was warm; on the low bottom land cold—note that the sun had set; when we mounted the little hill on which the hotel stands it was warm again. You can judge by this where wise men should locate themselves in California.

We left Escondido and its pleasant society with regret, and headed north over another pass, the roughest we had yet experienced, for on the further side we had to lock the hind wheels, and slide now as best we could into a long valley covered with mountain oak, carpeted with flowers, and on the low tracts of which the bamboo would grow luxuriantly. We forded the San Luis Rey river at noon, and lunched on a hill-side with an ostrich farm below us. It made me laugh to see the huge birds strutting in the sun, for I knew a Sunderland gentleman who walked exactly like them. Then over rolling uplands, up hill and down dale, we made our way to Fallbrook, reaching it in the only shower which has caught me so far in California.

Fallbrook has, in my judgment, incomparably the best climate we have met with on our journey. Situate 400 or 500 feet above the sea, it escapes frosts and dew. The air is dry and invigorating. The ocean breeze gives life. Grain and all manner of fruits grow luxuriantly. You may see there fields of maize on which no rain has ever fallen; Egyptian wheat which is cut down and comes again next season unsown, volunteer barley and

A JACK-RABBIT DRIVE. 2,500 BAGGED.

oats growing up for hay, and on the lower hill-sides and in the vales oranges, lemons, and all manner of fruit. It was at Prohibition Fallbrook that the greatest rebuff of our lives met us. We could not, in the hotel, borrow even a corkscrew, though only to open a modest bottle of Apollinaris Water! So sternly teetotal were they that one of us had to go out and buy the convenient article in a store.

After staying there a day for exploration we headed still for the north, climbed another mountain pass into a range of mountain-valleys, known as the Vallecitos (the Little Valleys) of Temecula, and descended their northern slope into the Temecula Valley. Here we drew rein. What a scene was there! Far in front spread the valley with its rolling foot-hills, and beyond reared itself the giant range of the Bernardino Mountains shrouded in snow glistening in the glorious sun. There, on the left, was Old Baldy eighty miles away, above Los Angeles. For a hundred miles the snow-capped peaks repeated themselves till the eyes rested on Mount Bernardino itself, rising two miles sheer from its surrounding plain, and further east on noble San Jacinto and San Felipe, twin guardians of the Arizona desert. Not even in the Alps have my eyes rested on a mountain landscape more wide-extending or more majestically grand.

CHAPTER IX.

A MOUNTAIN SHEEP-RANCH — THE HAPPY VALLEY — RAIN —THE PALA MISSION—AN INDIAN CHIEF OF A NEW TYPE—THE GREAT MESA—COYOTES AT LAST—SCOTLAND AND CALIFORNIA—A GOLD FEVER AND ITS ISSUE—TYPICAL LAND SALE—AN OX ROASTED—ITS ROASTERS ROASTED TOO.

Brewster Hotel, San Diego,
March 10th, 1889.

WE took advantage of our presence in the Temecula Valley to pay a promised visit to Mr. Parker Dear at his mountain ranch, Santa Rosa. Years ago Mr. Dear's father bought the estate for a small sum, and here the son lives with his charming Spanish wife, literally monarch of all he surveys. He met us with his team at Wildomar, a small roadside station, and with hearty welcome convoyed us to his mountain home. Our route rose through a wooded glen till, at 1700 feet above the sea, Santa Rosa Ranch lay before us; verdant valleys, edged by rolling hills crowned with evergreen oaks, and amongst which scattered boulders of enormous size lent added picturesqueness to the scene. Santa Rosa is one of the few remaining upland cattle-ranches of the county. It covers 47,000 acres, 15,000 of which have been recently sold to a land company. The remaining 32,000 acres Mr. Dear amuses himself with farming, running between 2000 and 3000 head of cattle, and growing a certain quantity of grain. His pretty ranch-house, set by some springs on the edge of a charming ravine, opened its welcoming doors to us just as evening drew nigh. Standing upon the portico, amidst roses and flowering shrubs, the cultivated fields in front of us, the hills, covered with a rich greensward rising beyond, and groves of noble

SANTA ROSA. PARKER DEAR, ESQ.

evergreen oaks filling in the picture, we might easily have dreamed ourselves into the belief that we were gazing on a Devonshire scene in midsummer. A glance at the shadowy palms, however, and at the orange-trees laden with their golden fruit, recalled to us the fact that we were in California, 1700 feet above the sea, in February, innocent of great-coats, and armed with hats only against the sun. The voices of the children of the house, mingling English and Spanish phrases, broke in upon the silence with odd effect, fitting in with the cooing of doves and croaking of noisy frogs; but all forgotten when a barbaric gong called us to dinner and to the presence of a Chinese cook and serving-man, whose clear-cut ascetic face (different, indeed, from the ordinary coarse Mongol type) reminded one of a Roman cardinal. We spent the two next days in driving round our host's domain, thoro'-bush, thoro'-brier, over many a swelling hill, through many a smiling valley, by devious tracks and rocky passes. The deer, ancient denizens of these cool retreats, had vanished, but in their stead cattle crowned the hills, or lolled by the side of crystal streamlets in the vales. No need for fence to hedge them in; the towering hills around were their sure guardians; apart from these one solitary gate across the road we entered by sufficed. What scenes of quiet pastoral beauty! Surely the grim old doctor was mistaken; the Happy Valley of Rasselas was *not* in Abyssinia.

On the evening of the second day, from a mountain top, we had a view of the distant ocean and the whole coast-line stretching down to San Diego and the Mexican hills. A little cloud, bigger than a man's hand, was just discernible on the far southern horizon. "It will be rain to-morrow," said our host, "perhaps to-night." We listened with incredulous ears, for not another cloud dimmed the wide expanse. But the prophet was right. As the sun set the light cavalry of the storm came hurrying up, and soon the main battalia, dark and dense, blotted out the stars and banked themselves against the northern mountains. At nine the rain came down in more than downright English fashion; the wind and it made merry all the night; and when morning came the clouds hid the hills and the mists swirled fantastically amongst the weeping oaks. We realised at last that even in the Land of the Sun they sometimes have bad weather. We drove through it, however, without distress, and in the outer valley found again the sun.

Mounted on our waggon, our road lay eastward along the foot-hills till we struck the Pala Pass, up and down which we drove for the San Luis River. This pass is, I think, the grandest of those we traversed. In it we saw for the first time what a Californian mountain side is like when thick-carpeted with the Californian poppy. It is one sloping mass of golden glory. On the banks of the San Luis we found the Pala Mission built by the Spanish Jesuits. It is one of the antiquities of California, yet is but a century old; so very new is the land. The dried-clay walls are crumbling; the Fathers are gone; the broken cloisters, which once echoed now to the sound of sacred song and again to the fierce cries of wild onlookers at bull-fights and bear-baits, contained nought but some shy-faced Indian children and a few straggling hens. Only the bronze bells survived intact to tell of a livelier past. Yet more remains. All down the valley we came upon Indian families living in their wooden cabins and tilling the fruitful earth. One of the chiefs had quite a pleasant home, surrounded by an orange grove and a well-kept orchard and fields green with barley and oats. Gone his predatory habits, if not his predatory instincts, for evermore! Uncle Sam's marshal is master here. Thank the Fathers, then, for something attempted, something done.

We crossed the river (now in flood) by a wooden bridge some miles further down, traversed the Montserrat Ranch, owned by the Alvarados, who are descended, it is said, from one of the famous companions of Cortes, then struck up one of the passes to the south, and came by Buena Vista and San Marcos back by another route to sweet Escondido. Another cloudless day saw us careering through the Barnardo Valley, skirting the fine Vale of Poway, and climbing the mesa beyond. There what was to me the greatest surprise of the journey struck our eyes. Stretched out before us, 400 or 500 feet above the sea, was a huge, unexpected expanse of country, covering from 60,000 to 90,000 acres, with grand views of mountain and of sea; flat apparently as a pancake; thickly covered with scrub of sage and grease-wood; rich and fertile of soil; running to within a mile or two of the great city of San Diego; and yet useless—useless for lack of water! Let but enterprise bring the water from the mountains, and this widespreading waste will be as the Garden of the Lord. Sufficiently above the sea to escape the frosts, sufficiently near it to catch in their freshness the daily ocean-breezes, there is no product of the temperate or sub-tropical zones which you cannot raise here, and raise with such profusion as amply to repay the labour of man. Upon this mesa our sportsman had his first and only shot at the Californian wolf. All the way we had kept our eyes open for these slinking thieves. Here, at least, three of them emerged from a small canon, and showed themselves for a moment amongst the bush 400 yards off. The distance proved, alas, too much for the Winchester or its wielder, and the coyotes were too politic to give him a second chance. Evening saw us safe in the comfortable Brewster, and our horses at rest in their stable. We had been pleasant companions for between 300 and 400 miles.

Do you ask me why I have described this tour at such length, particularising all these unknown places, setting down these strange unpronounceable names? I will tell you. You get off (at least the lucky ones among you) to the Cumbrian Hills or Wales or fair Scotland or (the luckiest of you) to Switzerland, and you revel there in the summer weather and return for the fogs and slush. Now, I want you to realise that here, in Southern California, there are valleys as fair, passes as grand, mountains as noble, peaks of Alpine sublimity and grandeur ; and you may wander among them without discomfort, nay, with real pleasure, in November, December, January, escape for good the nipping north-easters and the choking fogs, and enjoy your own homes in the gay summer-time. I speak, as I said, to the lucky ones. But even as I write the vision rises before me of crowds ill-fed, badly clothed, badly housed, in our great northern cities. Ah, my brothers! Would that the yellow lamp before me were Aladdin's lamp! One touch upon its magic surface, and you too should taste the comforts of a land where bounteous Nature does so much to abate the ills of life. You too should learn that

> "There are hills beyond Pentland,
> And lands beyond Forth."

When we returned to San Diego we found the city labouring under two excitements—one small, the other severe. Gold had been found at Ensenada, fifty miles over the Mexican border, in Lower California. Gold! Nuggets, dust, nuggets, dust! That produced the severe excitement. All the town was agog. Men talked of nothing else. You had but to get a shovel and a pan, and be off to the mines, and you were rich for life. It is true you would do well to take a horse, for eighty miles over the pathless mountains is no joke; and a revolver, for law is not omnipotent amongst the lawless; and blankets or a tent, for of shelter there is none; and food for man and beast, since it can't be bought save at famine prices, even if at all. Still—gold, magic gold, for the digging of it! Hundreds went, nay, hundreds more came from far-off places and went. Even the waiters in some of the hotels rushed off to seek fortune. All the have-nots struck south. We debated whether we too should go and see this great sight. But as the discomforts were apparent, and, like the steward in the parable, we could not dig, we decided on the whole that we would stay at home and read about it. We did well. For the whole thing was a fraud, a sham. Of gold there proved to be little, and the only persons who made much were not the gallant diggers, but the astute traders who took down the necessaries of life, and sold them for what they chose to ask. The sham is now exploded. One more gold-craze has vanished into curses both loud and deep.

The mild excitement was over a land-sale. Of land-sales at large and town-sites, and Californian folly therein, I may write more by-and-by. Here it may be sufficient to prove that land-jobbers have wily ways in other lands than ours if I reproduce the advertisement, which I trust the good foreman-printer will set out, if not in letters quite as large as the original, still so that it may catch men's eyes—

ROASTED OX!
SATURDAY, FEBRUARY 23RD,
THERE WILL BE
BARBECUED
A fine Young Steer on the Campus of
SAN DIEGO COLLEGE OF LETTERS
AT PACIFIC BEACH.
He will be carved and served to the Hungry Throng at 12 o'clock. Ladies will be served in the College Dining Hall, and the gentlemen under the shining canopy of heaven.
Upon this occasion there will be a continuation of the
IMMOLATION SALE
Of Real Estate by the San Diego College of Letters Company.
CHOICE RESIDENCE AND VILLA SITES
Will be sold to the highest bidder. The sale does not affect the schedule price of this property, but is made at this time to meet the pressing need of San Diego's Institution of Learning.
TERMS OF SALE.—10 per cent. cash; balance in 30 days. Title clear of mortgages and taxes.
SPECIAL EXCURSIONS!
Trains will leave D Street Motor Depot at 9 and 10 A.M., 1.30 P.M. Fare for round trip, 25c.
The sale will be announced at 11 A.M. by the sweet notes of the Bugle Call.
Come and spend a day in San Diego's most lovely and classical suburb.

Ye gods! If a College of Letters must rear its front sacred to Truth and Learning by miserable lying trade-puffing like this, shall not Wisdom hide her head! I am thankful to say little land was sold, despite the Roasted Ox; perhaps *because* of him, for doubtless he was tough and burnt or underdone. I said—lying. Why, I visited (not on sale day) this " most lovely and classical suburb of San Diego." A bare, treeless slope of clay and sand, a wooden hotel untenanted, a few commonplace wooden dwellings scattered here and there; no avenues, no gardens, no cliff, no point or place of interest made by man or left by God save the yellow sea-sands and the rolling sea. Hear you, how it roars at your lies! Oh, Fathers of the College of Letters, Heaven forgive you! no one else can. A fine, truth-loving, truth-telling set of pupils you'll rear in your college if ever you get it. Hear a plain man: San Diego may get along without learning; it can't get along at all without men who speak the modest truth. Barbecue no more oxen, my friends; tell no more—tarradiddles.

A CALIFORNIAN ROSEBUSH.

CHAPTER X.

THE LAND BOOM AND ITS EFFECTS—LONDON ECLIPSED ON PAPER—WORK VERSUS SPECULATION—SANTA BARBARA—A WESTERN RIVIERA—INTERVIEW WITH FRIARS OF ORDERS BROWN—THE OJAI VALLEY—A WONDROUS WEATHER RECORD—STORM AT LAST—BACK TO SAN DIEGO—MR. ALBERT GREY—FINAL DRIVES—FLOWERS AND BIRDS—ROAD-RUNNERS AND RATTLESNAKES—A HOMERIC CONTEST—A COMMONPLACE ONE—HO FOR ENGLAND!—MR. ALBERT GREY AT SEA.

Brewster Hotel, San Diego,
March 25th, 1889.

ANXIOUS to see somewhat of the country north of Los Angeles, we left here by train for Santa Barbara, 100 miles north-west of that city, and 230 miles north-north-west from San Diego. Even so small a space could not conveniently be covered in one day, for the trains do not run at more than twenty to twenty-five miles an hour, and do not fit in. Indeed, it took us four days to reach our objective, for we halted in Los Angeles and Pasadena. The land there looked richer and greener than ever, as the crops showed more above ground, and the orchards now in bloom were lovely to behold. Upon this journey we realised more fully the inordinate folly of the people in the matter of town-sites. When the "boom" was on two years and a half ago, nearly every one who had or could acquire an estate of any size was convinced that a town could be galvanised into existence on it. Townsites were laid out; white stakes marked out thousands, nay, tens of thousands of house-plots; avenues and streets were designed, and rows of trees planted; public auction sales were held with bands and banners and free lunches and roasted oxen; men would stand in a *queue* through the livelong night to get the first turn in the morning, or, better still, hire the impecunious for ten or twenty dollars to keep their turns for them; nor was it uncommon for these lucky ones to get their plots and sell them forthwith to the eager, crack-brained enthusiasts at the tail of the *queue* for a substantial profit. California was mad.

To add to, if not to create the madness, the professional land-boomers from the East trooped in with their carpet-bags. These gentry exploit the "booms" just as regularly and religiously as our English betting-men frequent successive race-courses. They are now whilst I write off to Washington territory, where there is another boom. They bought and sold, ran up prices, fanned the fire, puffed and boasted, and finally moved off with full pockets, taking good care that whoever was left *they* were not. A modest computation has been made that in San Gabriel and its adjoining valleys alone sufficient town-sites were laid out to accommodate a population equal to the aggregate of the trifling little cities of London, Paris, Berlin, St. Petersburg, Vienna, and New York! The whole thing was a manifest, a gigantic folly. You may call cities from the vasty deep, but they won't come. Most of the projects fell still-born. I visited, for instance, the great paper-city of Huntingdon. There were the white stakes and the house-plots, and the avenues and the budding rows of trees, and—one wooden shanty to grace the whole. I saw in a veracious newspaper that Arcadia had had quite an access of prosperity, and would soon have to apply for incorporation as a city of the second class. I drove over to Arcadia. Ten buildings of wood or brick! Ten, on my honour, and no more! You can yet see vineyards running wild (cut up into lots), orchards unpruned (cut up into lots), orange groves dying (cut up into lots). Gentlemen have been pointed out to me who gave at the rate of 2500 dollars and more per acre for their lands, and would gladly get rid of them at almost any price. The "boom," like all fevers, did more harm than good. The few astute ones might make money, the gullible many are left with properties held at unreal prices, and generally mortgaged at 10 per cent. or upwards. I never saw so many "land-poor" men in my life. You might imagine they were all Irish landlords.

Men are of course wiser now, taught by bitter experience. They realise that the wealth of California is in the land; that this wealth can be easily got out of it by work, and not otherwise; that therefore they must plant and not gamble in corner lots, dig and not fool away time and money and peace of mind at barbecues. Stakes are being shamefacedly pulled out and burnt, hedges trimmed, trees and vines tended. Land, too, is slowly but surely falling to its true value, and will again tempt many a frugal hardworking settler whom inordinate prices forced elsewhere. Despite the "boom," not because of it, Southern California will flourish.

Somewhat too much of these matters into which the dollar ceaselessly enters. But, indeed, it is a favourite taunt against these climate-blessed, easy-going Californians that their whole talk is of dollars, and their sole amusement gambling in corner lots. I can say better things of them than that. If they talk dollars, they build churches and schools. Every little village, as every large town, must have these and a sufficiency of them. There is a story told of one ambitious little settlement, the inhabitants whereof, having obtained church and school, sat in solemn conclave to consider what other adjunct of civilisation they might next secure. They resolved on having a hearse—a real hearse with orthodox ornaments and waving plumes. It was ordered, and in due course its approach notified. As the Israelites turned out to meet the ark, so the settlers went forth to meet their hearse, headed by their brass band. The band (so the story goes) could play but one tune, and to the cheerful lilt of "Wait for the waggon, and we'll all take a ride," the hearse was safely housed, the villagers proudly feeling that for them, at any rate for the present, the resources of civilisation *were* exhausted.

Amusements, too, they have. For the second time in thirty years I visited a race-course, tempted by the announcement of a race between a young man and a young woman.

I found a considerable crowd, adorned by fewer blackguards than I anticipated. The course was a smooth oval of a mile. Each competitor had four horses ready saddled on it. The man had to mount one of his, ride once round, jump off, ride the second round, and so on, horse by horse and mile by mile, till the full distance of ten miles had been covered. The young woman had to do likewise, save that she was lifted from horse to horse in a man's arms. It was really an exciting business, and no horse was punished. It may interest the ladies to learn that their champion won by a quarter of a mile, doing the ten miles in twenty-one minutes twenty-six seconds. Another Californian amusement which I did not honour with my presence is set out in an advertisement which announces—

"A SLAUGHTERING EXHIBITION.

"Whereat ten butchers are pitted against each other to demonstrate who can slay oxen and sheep most painlessly and with greatest expedition. ADMISSION, 10 CENTS."

I do not know how many attended this brutalising exhibition. But sure I am that to estimate the people at large by such a sample would be unfair; just as unfair as it is for the Rev. Sam. Jones to go from city to city and declare each in turn *the wickedest city* in the whole world. I daresay there are enough, and more than enough, of brutal and base folk here as elsewhere, and one is not allowed to forget it is a new land where all sorts come. But these Southern Californians seem to me to smack of the genial climate; if a trifle keen in business, they are decent and sensible in their amusements; they delight in little social gatherings, musical entertainments and lectures, and love the open hill-sides and the ocean sands.

One common charge against them I must refute, if only in gratitude for many kindnesses. I was told they were a drinking if not a drunken people. The wits delight to retail to "tender-feet" (that's the cant name for outlanders like myself) the standing joke of a gentleman entering one of the huge railway cars and crying out "Is there a

SANTA BARBARA MISSION.

Californian here?" whereupon every Californian sprang to his feet and produced his pocket corkscrew. He knew what he was wanted for. The wits may have reason; all. I can say is that, after three months' experience amongst all classes, I think them, with exceptions, a temperate race. In that space of time I have only seen three drunken men: one was a Californian, another an Englishman, and the third an Irishman who would persist in declaring himself Scotch—only when he was drunk his brogue betrayed him.

Now for Santa Barbara. Our course from Los Angeles lay first to the north, through the Fernando Valley to Saugus, and thence west down Santa Clara Valley and by the sea-shore. Here the great San Bernardino Range, which I spoke of as running west from the Sierra Nevadas to the sea, approaches close to the coast, which itself bends in from Point Conception and runs east. Between the mountains and the sea is a narrow strip only a few miles wide. Santa Barbara County consists of this coast-strip and the mountains and the valleys therein. The town itself is prettily situate on the coast, and has a more completed aspect than most of the other towns. Its district is proudly called the Riviera of California. Sheltered by the mountains from the north, and sloping south to the peaceful sea, it invites the comparison conveyed in the name, but one misses alike the historical associations and the glorious sea cliffs of its European prototype, though, to be fair, one must admit that the islands in the offing, rising grandly to 2500 feet, present counterbalancing attractions not to be despised. Santa Barbara is held in much repute by American physicians as a refuge for persons afflicted with lung troubles, being free from those enormous variations of temperature which afflict our Riviera. Its air struck me, however, as more humid and relaxing than any I had yet encountered in this land, corresponding in this respect with that of Funchal in Madeira, where the contiguity of mountain and sea develops every evening a humidity dangerous to the weak. I may be wrong as to this. I was there in the brief wet season; it may probably be different all the rest of the year. In that case let the Barbarians forgive me.

The most interesting and noticeable feature of the place is the Mission, one of the few remaining in good repair. It stands upon the mesa, with a magnificent view of sea, islands, and mountains, and with its white walls and dark red roofs is quaintly attractive. We drew up in a passing shower, and entered the plain and rather commonplace church, over the east door of which is a death's-head with cross-bones, not of stone however. Some grimly realistic friar had picked up in the churchyard a grinning skull and a couple of bones, which once were helpful to some son of Adam, and had fixed them in the plaster to appal one's skipping spirits. From the church we passed to the monastery and rang the bell. An aged friar in brown appeared. Could we see the place? No; it was not permitted. Something in the cut of his face and turn of his tongue caught my attention. "Why," said I, "you are an Irishman." "Shure, and I am." "From what place?" "Why, from Derry." "Did he know Strabane?" "Shure, and I do." And then he and I fell into reminiscences, and in five minutes he thought we *could* see the house; he would seek the superior. That reverend father soon appeared. Irish too! From Youghal he. Did I know Youghal and Cappoquin, and the lovely Blackwater and Lismore? Of course I did; and his rotund form loomed larger, and his round jolly face, crowned with jet black hair, was wreathed in smiles. Friar Tuck we christened him on the spot, and when we entered the old refectory, with its white-washed walls and uneven earthen floor and smoke-blackened roof, it need not have much astonished us if the Holy Clerk had introduced us to the Black Sluggard himself. So old-world-like, so romantic was the darkened room! The garden behind was ill-kept, but contained some noticeable trees. The cloister wall to the rear had fallen, not to be reared again. We talked with our jolly friar of things at large, of the Spanish Founders, of the lovely land and weather, of Ireland and of Parnell. "Far from the madding crowd,"

THE IRISH MONK.

he knew of and was deeply interested in the Irish struggle and the Irish leader. What Irishman worthy of the name would not be? We bade him adieu with hearty handshakes, and since I left I have sent him the *Times* with the full account of Pigott's cross-examination, flight, and fate. May the Saints forgive him if he enjoyed it just for one night better than his prayers!

Our intention was to have driven from Santa Barbara across the mountains to Monterey. But the weather was changeable, and all things pointed to a rain-storm. We therefore returned by train thirty miles east to San Buena Ventura, and drove up the lovely Ventura to the still lovelier Ojai (Oh-hi) Valley. A place of peace and beauty, a vale shut in by mountains, and filled with thousands, tens of thousands, of spreading ever-green oaks, amidst which the white dwellings of the settlers are scattered about. The weather record for this district shows that they had thirty bright, rainless days in October, twenty-five in November, twenty-four in December, twenty-nine in January, and twenty-four in February! Ah! your eyes shine with envy, you English folk, growling amidst your sleet and slush. Pray be comforted to know that even amidst such perfect surroundings I caught a nose-rending influenza, ending in low fever, which drove me to bed, and was only exorcised by copious doses of the favourite Californian remedy, quinine. We loved Ojai, but, storm-warned, hurried back to Ventura, and so to Los Angeles. There the storm burst. Before I came to California I was told there was no fog here, no thunder, no lightning, no hydrophobia. Fogs we have had, though no wet ones. Now for four days and nights it rained almost without intermission, with thunder, lightning, and hail. Roads were washed out, railway bridges carried away, all traffic was suspended, whilst we moped in our hotel, feeling that if only a Californian dog would go mad all our fond illusions would have vanished together.

As soon as the weather permitted we returned to San Diego. There a pleasant surprise was in store for us in the form of a visit from Mr. Quilter, M.P., and Mr. Albert

Grey, who was accompanied by his cousin, Sir Edward's younger brother. All seemed vigorous and strong, Mr. Albert Grey especially looking brown and ruddy, and plumper than I have ever seen him. He and I had not met since the declaration of the poll in the Tyneside Division in 1886. Then we were unfortunately political opponents. Now we met with friendly greeting and good-humouredly chatted over old-time strife. He thought the defeat at Kennington, of which news had just reached us, a serious blow, but had no thought of surrender; the Tories *would* not grant Home Rule, and if they wanted to, they *should* not. I laughed at the idea of Whigs preventing Tories from making progress. And he laughed too, but he won't budge. Like Macbeth he cries—

"Ring the alarum bell, blow wind, come wrack,
At least we'll die with harness on our back."

We have spent the last week of our sojourn in further drives, visiting Spring Valley and the Jamul Ranch, and sweet Poway, Barnardo, and the lower Dieguito Valley. Details of these excursions I spare you. The country is now one wide expanse of richest verdure, adorned with a wealth of wild flowers which I am powerless to describe. Many a time I have wished that my botanising friend, John Cameron, had been with me, only he would have been continually losing himself in his hunt after flowers, and there are no bellmen here. Of some of the beasts and birds I have spoken. Amongst the latter, the golden lark, with his rich melodious notes, the capricious mocking-bird, the impudent blue-jay, and the butcher-bird, which hunts mice and sticks them up on thorns till he is ready to devour them, are constant sources of interest and amusement. But the most curious of all is the road-runner, a bird about the size of a pheasant, long-legged and long of bill, with a brown breast and crested head. He is the sworn foe of snakes, and they tell me a fight between him and a rattlesnake is a sight to see. Espying his formidable enemy, he gathers the sharp spikes of the prickly cactus, and plants them barrier-like around him;

nor can the snake escape or rear himself to strike without sharp and painful wounds. Seeing him thus entangled, the road-runner goes in like a game-cock, pecks at him, leaps warily back from the poisoned fangs, and literally worries the brute to death.

I have, alas! not witnessed such a Homeric combat. A rattlesnake, however, I have met; one, and I don't wish to meet another. We were driving down from Jamul last Friday evening, when we espied him in the track. Whilst one held the horses, the four others of us jumped down. Sticks we had none, and not a stone was to be had. The young sportsman of the party possessed himself of the whip, and the rest of us gathered pieces of hard clay. Thus armed, we advanced to the attack. The clay broke innocuously on him, and two ineffectual blows of the whip only turned him on us in fury, his eye glittering wickedly, and his fierce rattle sounding the assault. Just as he reared for a spring, a fortunate third blow from the whip broke his back six inches above the rattle, and he turned tail and wriggled into the brush, his rattle marking the line of retreat. We followed cautiously, and a few more well-delivered blows crushed his ugly head and terminated the maleficent career of at any rate one enemy of progress. We tied a shoestring round his neck, rolled him into the horse-pail, forded the Sweetwater River with the water running through our waggon, took advantage of the time to fill the pail with water so that the wriggling wretch might drown if he would not die like a gentleman, and carried him as a trophy into San Diego. He measures four feet five and a half inches, is now being fitted with a new inside, and will doubtless appear by-and-by as a specimen in some English museum.

On Monday I leave for home.

P.S.—Just as I am gathering my possessions together for a start I learn from the newspapers that Mr. Albert Grey has gone down to Lower or Mexican California, and had an exhilarating adventure. It would appear that in landing at Ensenada he, and Uncle Sam's mail-bags along with him, fell into the sea. They were, happily, fished out, and, says the veracious reporter, "after being put through the drying machine were none the worse for their wetting." I presume he meant the bags, but Western reporters sacrifice all things to spiciness. Mr. Grey, I have learned since, is all right and jolly, whereat political friends and foes will alike rejoice.

WINTER BATHING IN THE PACIFIC.

CHAPTER XI.

WESTERN NEWSPAPERS — THE "BOOM" — PAPERS AND THEIR ODDITIES — AN UNIQUE ADVERTISEMENT — THE PARAGONS OF EDITORS—MR. POTT REDIVIVUS—O'BRIEN'S HEAD OFF— PATTERN REPORTING — WESTERN HUMOUR — OLD FOES MEET — SOMETHING FOR THE LAWYERS — SOMETHING, TOO, FOR THE TEETOTALERS—THE LADIES NOT FORGOTTEN—A COSTLY COFFIN—WIVES TO THE FRONT—SULPHUR SAM'S WARNING.

Del Mar, March 28th, 1889.

THESE discursive sketches would seem, to me at any rate, lacking in any completeness they may be presumed to attain, if they take no note of the newspapers of the Far West. In California alone there are no less than 411 among a population of a million and a half; whilst the contiguous States and Territories probably muster as many more. The papers of San Francisco are admirable productions, sufficing both as to quantity and quality, and some of those of the other large towns are not much behind. But every place of any importance or ambition must have a paper of its own. Especially must the towns which are being "boomed" into existence have their weekly organs, in which every trivial fact down to the exact weight of the new-born babies, as well as every incident which may seem to excite interest in the place, is duly and diffusely chronicled. Some of the editors are easy-going enough, as, for instance, the gentleman who the other week apologised for the late and incomplete issue of his paper, because "We have been engaged in planting out and improving our ten-acre tract," but others have the keenest eye for the main chance. Last week's Bethlehem *Pealler* (Phœbus, what a name!) contains the following advertisement—

"MOTHERS, FATHERS,

"HUSBANDS WHO INTEND TO BECOME FATHERS, LOOK AT THIS OFFER AND WEEP FOR JOY.

"The owners and projectors of the town of Bethlehem will give to the first child born in Bethlehem the garden spot of Santa Clara county, one lot on the principal street of said town, just as soon as we can ascertain the name of said child, and we don't care whether it is born in a manger or in the open air. We do know the offer is free for all, and open to all competitors. Those of you who are thinking seriously of having one will do well to grasp at this offer, for every child is not born with a silver spoon in its mouth."

Another "boomer" puffs thus—

"CHANEY COAL.

"A HOME PRODUCT THAT IS WINNING ITS WAY.

"The Chaney mine at Elsinore has now fairly established its claim as a permanent industry of this section of the State. Ten tons per day are used in this city, the same amount shipped to other points, and about the same amount used in the manufacture of sewer pipe, and in other ways in and about Elsinore."

Imagine the twinkling eyes and merry smile with which Lord Durham or Mr. Baker Forster would greet the announcement of a new "permanent industry" in the shape of a colliery which actually draws thirty tons a-day. Of Murrieta I must tell a story. Two years or more ago, when it was "booming," a good friend of mine visited it, on the very day of all days when the hotel cat kittened. He took a fancy to the lively twins, and had them sent off in a basket to his home in San Diego. Next issue of the local "boomer" announced—

"Murrieta flourishes. Quite a new industry has sprung up in our midst. Yesterday, Mr. Winchester, of San Diego, made his first consignment of cats to that city. We are going ahead."

I have seen, I suppose, fifty or a hundred of these little prints during the past three months. Each of them assures me that its particular locality is the richest, the most beautiful, the most salubrious, the most desirable, the most perfect place for settlement in all the wide world. How easy it is for truth to be transmuted into lies by the vulgar process of exaggeration! By piecing together morsels culled at intervals from their veracious pages, I think I can photograph the peculiarities and oddities of Western American life better perhaps than by pages of detailed description. I warn my readers, then, that the present chapter will be mainly the product of scissors and paste, and that I shall figure, like Autolycus, as "a mere picker-up of unconsidered trifles."

What of the editors to begin with? Well, I am in no doubt about the Southern Californian ones at any rate. Quite recently they held a great gathering in Los Angeles, and here is the modest editorial description of them in the Los Angeles *Times*—

"The handsome, witty, able, learned, and wealthy gentlemen that assembled in this city yesterday under the name of 'The Editorial Association of Southern California' comprise, it is unnecessary to say, nearly all the brains in the Sixth Congressional district of this State. They were seventy-eight, and they represented about half a hundred newspapers; but these ideas of number are utterly inadequate to any representation of the power they wield and the influence they possess. To them, in great part, is confided the destiny of Southern California; for it is not too much to say that the newspapers have more to do with the prosperity of the country than any other agency."

The editors are doubtless smart fellows, but I am bound to say they sometimes lose their temper like common folk; as witness the following editorial for which this same *Times* was responsible just about the same date, and which recalls the palmiest days of Eatanswillian literary Billingsgate—

"WITH OUR COMPLIMENTS.

"Some vicious, virulent, and villainous street tattler—employed, evidently, to do the dirty work of a notorious fakir and proved scoundrel whom the *Times* has justly held up to public execration and contempt, and whose trail the sheriff has been following like a sleuth-hound, and who is even now in a state of collapse—is pacing around, we are informed, shooting off his mud-filled, hired mouth against the *Times*, ostensibly because it called attention—without money, without price, and without solicitation—to the solid and thriving condition of one of our leading financial institutions, ascribing to us improper motives in so doing. That is a very foolish and impotent, as well as a very vicious, charge to make, you tool of a scoundrel! The

Times is in the habit of drawing public attention, without money and without price, to those financial and commercial features of Los Angeles which are peculiarly sound, strong, and meritorious, for the sake of the truth and its effect upon people at home and abroad; for the sake of the best interests of the city, whose prosperity we, in common with other good citizens, are labouring to promote. And we have no apology to make to anybody—much less to cowards, scoundrels, embezzlers, pretenders, fakirs, and their ready tools—for our course in that regard. No successful attack can be made upon our motives; it is too late in the day for those base tactics; they are the resort of desperate men, in a desperate plight, struggling in a desperate and hopeless cause. They cannot win. What would these low-bred cattle—these political mustangs and social scrubs—have us do? Would they have us proclaim to the world that our banks, or any of them, are wildcat concerns, on the eve of collapse, like the fakirs themselves? Go to, cattle! We shall pursue the even tenor of our way, and continue to 'do the State (and city) some service.'"

And the *Colusa Herald* gives prominence to the following, which may be a joke, but is much more likely to be gospel truth—

"There is an editor north of here who will not lie even about a loathsome contemporary if he knows it. 'We wish,' he says in his last issue, 'to retract our statement of last week to the effect that the editor of our contemporary had been drunk twice recently. In reality he had been drunk but once. Five days intervened between the dates referred to, but it was only one drunk.'"

Our literary guides make odd mistakes, too, or their compositors do. In another Los Angeles paper (I forget which) appeared the following note—

"The Soldiers' Home at Santa Monica is going on apace in the work of getting up the buildings. In a very short time they will be thrown open to the veterans, who will be glad to rest their *battle-scared* limbs by the side of the sunset sea, and to pass their declining years under the genial influences of our matchless climate."

"Battle-scared" is good; but it pales its ineffectual fires before the effulgence of this other Los Angelian brightness—

"The harsh and brutal treatment of William O'Brien, who is confined in Ballingham Gaol for what is termed a political offence, is on a par with the past shameful attempts to govern Ireland by the 'mother country.' Here we have a physically delicate man, an

AN ADOBÉ DWELLING.

educated gentleman, and ex-member of the British Parliament, seized by the constables, taken to gaol, stripped of his clothing, forcibly held while *his head is shaved off*—and then he is left with scant covering for twenty-four hours, upon the cold floor of his dismal prison cell. His sole offence is his patriotic defence of his oppressed countrymen. Perfidious England has many dark pages in the history of her intercourse with the world, but none that are more disgraceful as the story of her treachery, deceit, and cruelty in connection with the Irish race."

Poor William O'Brien must be badly fixed indeed with his head shaved off; though to judge from what I have lately read it is not, as a matter of fact, he, but some other people who have lost their heads.

The reporting staffs seem to be as jolly as the editors are wise.

"The staff of *The Post* was regaled last night with a recherche lunch, thoughtfully presented by Mr. Charles A. Dumbler. It consisted not only of a delicious collation of rare delicacies, but also included wine and cigars. The boys doff their hats, Charley."

It must have been under the baneful influence of this evening lunch that one of the reporters perpetrated the following enormity—

"A coloured damsel in a horrible state of intoxication split the atmosphere wide open early last night, at the corner of San Jacinto and Capitol Street, by the free use of her vigorous lungs. She was gathered in by the police, and during the journey to the caliboose she left a blue streak of imprecations in her wake."

For broad Western humour, however, you must consult that ubiquitous contributor to many journals,

THE ARIZONA KICKER.

"NEARING THE LIMIT.—We have been repeatedly asked why we did not open on the G. and S. railroad for its slow time, miserable cars, rough road, high rates, and generally incompetent service. It is because we have been expecting an annual pass from the road. We applied for it three months ago, but have heard nothing as yet. We are nearing the limit. If that pass is not here inside of a fortnight we shall sound our bugle in a way to make the officials of the road wish they had never been born."

"ONLY OUR WAY.—We understand that Colonel Colfax feels aggrieved because we referred to him last week as a dead-beat bum, who ought to be given a doze of White Cap medicine. The Colonel should not be so thin skinned. It's only our way of keeping track of the leaders of society."

"A FALSE ALARM.—A Chicago correspondent dropped in on us the other day for a brief visit, and after showing him our Washington hand-press, six varieties of job type, and two bundles of print paper, we took him out for a survey of the town. The news had gone abroad that he was a Chicago detective, and it was laughable to note the effect upon our leading citizens. A dozen or more broke for the sage brush, without stopping for clean shirts, and so many others cut off their whiskers or donned false ones that we walked the whole length of Apache Avenue without meeting a man we could recognise at first glance.

"While there is nothing mean about us, this is a feature we are going to work about twice a month on this town. It will keep the boys unsettled and anxious, and may be the means of converting some of them from the error of their ways. It's an awful good feeling to feel that you are the only man in a town of 3000 people whose liver don't kick the breath out of him every time a stranger comes along and takes a second look at the bridge of your nose."

"WE COME DOWN.—We stated our belief last week that our contemporary, which is eternally bragging about its increase of circulation, did not print 150 copies weekly. We were honest in what we said. The old bristle-backed hyena who claims to be editor and publisher sent for us yesterday to examine his books and figure up circulation. We made the astounding discovery that he has a *bonâ-fide* circulation of 163 copies. When we are right we stick to the point, but we apologise for the thirteen copies."

Or what ails this veracious history of

THE WAYBACK TRAIN.

"I'll tell you a story, which, although not new, is tip-top:—On some roads in Wayback they attract a passenger to a freight train and call it 'mixed.' It is not in the order of things that such trains should travel very rapidly, and sometimes there is considerable growling among the passengers. On one of these trains a nervous man asked for the hundredth time, 'Are we most there, conductor? Remember my wife's sick, and I'm anxious.' 'We'll get there on time,' replied the conductor, stolidly. Half-an-hour later the nervous man approached the conductor again, saying, mournfully, ' I guess she's dead now. I'd give you a little something extra if you could manage to catch up with the funeral. Maybe she won't be so decomposed but what I would recognise her.' The conductor glared at him, and the man subsided. On the next round of the conductor, the man approached him in a determined way. 'Conductor, if the wind isn't dead ahead I wish you would put on some steam. I'd like to see where my wife is buried before the tombstone is crumbled to

SAN GABRIEL MISSION.

pieces. Put yourself in my place for a moment.' The conductor shook him off, and the man relapsed into profound melancholy. 'I say, conductor,' said he, after a long pause, 'I've got a note coming due in three months. Can't you fix it so as to rattle along a little?' 'If you come near me again I'll knock you down,' snorted the conductor, feeling that he was being guyed. The nervous man regarded him sadly, and went to his seat. Two hours later, the conductor, on his tour for tickets, found his man engaged in a game of cards, laughing and chatting pleasantly. 'Halloa, there,' said the conductor, 'you don't seem to feel so badly about your wife's death now.' 'No,' sighed the nervous man, as he put the winnings of a jackpot in his pocket, 'time heals all wounds—assuages all grief.' 'And you're not so particular about your note now, either?' sneered the conductor. 'No, not now,' answered the nervous man; 'I'm all right about the note. I've been figuring up, and find that the note is outlawed by the statute of limitation since I spoke to you last.'"

Now let us be serious again. Here is a Western picture of another sort. The Rev. Sam. Jones has been here evangelising. He held amongst other meetings one specially for the surviving veterans of both sides in the Great War. The newspapers thus describe the scene—

"Mr. Jones began by saying: 'Before I read the text will every veteran of the blue, every member of the Grand Army of the Republic present, stand a moment.' (About 500 men arose, amid great applause.) 'Now, will the former wearers of the grey stand.' (About 300 arose in response to this suggestion, and were greeted with prolonged applause.) 'I trust whatever may be the memories from Fort Sumter to Appomatox, whatever may be the memories of those fearful days, I thank God to-day, when the din and smoke of battle has blown away, that we may be brethren and friends. I hail with delight the day when we shall clasp hands from the lakes to the gulf, and from Boston to San Francisco, all over this country; when, people with the common interest and the common purpose to spread kindness and humanity over the world, we will grow better and wiser."

I tell you I should have liked to witness that curious demonstration that here at any rate—

"The war-drum has been muffled, the battle-flag been furled,
In the parliament of men, the federation of *this* world."

Here are two or three items for the lawyers. It may interest them to learn by perusal of the following ordinance that an extinct English custom still survives in California :—

ORDINANCE NO. 41.

"The Board of Supervisors of the County of San Diego do ordain as follows:—

"Section I. There is hereby levied upon each male person over twenty-one years and under fifty-five years of age, found in any of the Road Districts of said County of San Diego, a road poll tax of three dollars for the year 1889.

"Section II. Any person liable as aforesaid for a road poll tax may at his option, before the first day of June 1889, work out his road poll tax in conformity to the following regulations, but not otherwise—

"1. Each Road Overseer must ascertain the names of all persons in his district liable for a road poll tax as aforesaid, and require of each person so liable the performance of the labour, or the payment of the tax.

"2. Any person may, instead of paying such tax, perform two days' labour upon the highways and bridges of his district.

"3. Each person appearing must actually work eight hours each day, to be credited to him by the overseer or commissioner. For every hour unnecessarily lost, or idled away, he must be charged two hours, to be worked out on some other day to be designated by the overseer or commissioner. Any person may work by an able-bodied substitute."

Or this may take their fancy, the description of a scene only possible in a land where judges are elected by the popular vote, and bench and bar change places with kaleidoscopic rapidity—

"'Judge Rix,' said Judge Hornblower solemnly, yesterday morning, as the retiring justice and his successor stood together under the daïs of Police Court No. 1, 'I need not introduce you to the practitioners of this Court. Your previous service as Judge of this court—a position you filled with intelligence and honour—has been rewarded by the citizens of this city by your re-election.'

"Judge Hornblower then thanked the officers of the Court for the assistance they rendered him during the term.

"He then turned again to Judge Rix.

"'And now, sir,' he resumed, 'I resign my seat to you, and assure you and the public that I do so with pleasure. It is a hard position to fill—it has been laborious, but I may say that I tried to discharge the duties honestly and faithfully.'

"Judge Hornblower paused, grasped Judge Rix's hand, pointed to heaven, and impressively said: 'I now induct you to your seat, and as the Superior Judge of this universe will extend mercy to you and me, may He give you wisdom and kindness of spirit to be merciful to the young men of our city. Save them, if possible, from becoming criminals. Again thanking you all, gentlemen, I retire to assume my place in the ranks of the attorneys.'

"His ex-Honour grasped his present Honour's hand, and then left the bench.

"When he reached the level he turned and, with stately humility—as a deposed monarch might announce himself the humble subject of his successor—said:

"'And now, your Honour, I would ask you to fix the bail of D. C. Barker, charged with battery, for whom I appear.'

"Judge Rix fixed the bail at 100 dollars, and the attorneys of the Court ground their teeth as they realised that a new and formidable contestant had entered the lists to fight for the cream of the Police Court practice."

Lawyers and teetotalers will unite to admire the ease with which a verdict, even of murder, can be set aside in this very, very free land.

"THE LEE CHUCK CASE.

"A NEW TRIAL GRANTED BECAUSE THE JURORS TOOK WINE AT DINNER.

"Justice Works, of the Supreme Court, rendered a decision yesterday in the case of Lee Chuck, convicted for murder in the first degree for having shot and killed Len Yuen. Among the grounds for a new trial set forth by the defendant in his appeal is the charge that the jurors drank intoxicating liquors while deliberating on their verdict. The affidavits in the case state that about two hours before bringing in their verdict the jurors took claret at their dinner, and used a little burnt cognac in their coffee. The Court decided that as the charge is not denied no stronger case for the appellant could be presented, and on that ground the case was sent back for a new trial."

It is tolerably hard to get a man hanged here unless you lynch him.

I cannot think of closing my lucky-bag without drawing a trifling prize or two for my lady friends. Then ladies all, both great and small, contemplate the pomp any of you may attain to if only you happen to die as the wife of an American quack doctor.

"A COSTLY COFFIN.

"The body of Mrs. Catherine Teagle, wife of West Chester's famous coloured doctor, will be interred at that place to-morrow morning with more pomp than has attended any recent funeral in this locality. Mrs. Teagle died of a complication of disorders at midnight last Wednesday. By an arrangement made before her death she was to-day laid out in a coffin which she had ordered and inspected herself, and which will cost her wealthy husband the sum of 1000 dollars. In appearance it is an exact reproduction of the casket in which the body of the late Samuel J. Tilden was incased, and it comes from the same manufactory. The wood from which it is made is the very finest cedar that could be procured, heavily lined with highly-tested copper. The trimmings are of the finest satin, and the pillow on which the dead woman's head rests is hand-embroidered. Besides all this, an exquisite satin shroud has been ordered for the occasion, bits of colouring being introduced to relieve the whole of any ghastly effect.

"'I want it to be better than the one in which Henry Ward Beecher was buried,' said Dr. Teagle this morning. 'She was an excellent woman, and deserves an unexcelled home in the grave.'

"All the other arrangements for the funeral are upon a similar scale. The funeral director was given explicit instructions to spare no expense, and he has obeyed instructions. Fifty of the finest carriages have been engaged, and a sumptuous dinner provided for those who come from a distance.

"Mrs. Teagle was born a slave, but became free by the operations of the emancipation proclamation, and came North shortly thereafter. She was a woman of more than ordinary capacity, and, borrowing money, went into the millinery business. With her savings she bought up real estate, which increased in value and finally made her rich. In her own right she was worth about 100,000 dollars when she died. Dr. Teagle, whom she married twenty years ago, obtained a large practice as a root and herb doctor, and also amassed considerable money. To-day he has an extensive list of white and coloured patients, who will accept medical service from no other physician."

To hard-working matrons I commend the example of a Californian heroine—

"MRS. MEADE'S GREAT FEAT.
"SHE SOWS AND PLANTS 100 ACRES OF WHEAT AT SAN JACINTO.

"S. N. Meade and his estimable wife, who own a fine farm on the mesa, have put in about 240 acres of wheat this season, and are still ploughing. Mrs. Meade, not caring to do the housework for a hired man, concluded it was cheaper to hire a girl and do the ploughing herself. Knowing his wife enjoyed all outdoor exercise, Mr. Meade accepted the proposition, at the same time thinking that a few days of ploughing would satisfy his wife—that it would be too much for her to undertake; but there he was mistaken. They commenced about Thanksgiving, both having a four-horse team and a gang plough. Mrs. Meade, who tends to her own team, has,

PRESIDENT HARRISON.

up to date, ploughed and sown as much as her husband. Up to two years ago Mrs. Meade had never been on a farm, having been born and raised in a city. She is a refined and an intelligent lady, capable of conversing upon any subject from butter-making to high art, or the political issues of the day."

Whilst my young lady friends (Heaven bless them, and send them good husbands!) I must, ere the Pacific lulls me to rest on my virtuous couch, regale with the terrible deeds of

"SULPHUR SAM.

"WILLIAM EVANS SCOFIELD MUST GO TO CHURCH WITH THE SAME GIRL.

"He has Monopolised the Attentions of the Fairest Daughters of Summit, N.J., and the Young Men of that Town will not Stand it any Longer—He takes Girls to Church on a Non-Sectarian Plan.

"The local beaux of Summit, N.J., headed by one Sulphur Sam, are preparing a horrible but rather indefinite vengeance for William E. Scofield, of this city, who persists in making himself agreeable to all the girls at once.

"William Evans Scofield, of One Hundred and Twenty-third Street, is thinking of applying for a permit to carry a gun. He is a slender, dapper young man, who wears his full name and good clothes on dress occasions ; and up in Summit, N.J., where he has been a visitor and a favourite with the girls ever since he was a boy, 3500 people are excited over the tragic possibilities of his reappearance, for recently his uncle, James H. Green, the upholsterer, received a letter as follows :

'OFFICE OF SULPHUR SAM, THE ROAD AGENT,
Dec. 21, 1888.

'*Mr. Green:*

'You had better warn W. E. Scofield to let Summit boys take Summit girls to church. If he does not keep out of town he will die the death of a dog. This is the first warning ; one more will come before the fatal end appears. Yours in blood, gall, and gore, SULPHUR SAM.'

" Mr. Scofield, on Thursday, received this in blood-red ink :

'*W. E. Scofield:*

'This is the last warning to keep out of Summit. I say no more, but take warning I say. NO NAME.'

"At five o'clock last evening a lot of young men and young women of Summit met at the Post Office to talk over these mysterious letters, which had just been published. When the crowd grew so large that the postmistress had to drive them off, an overflow meeting was held in Alec Taylor's drug store next door, over which 'Irv,' the clerk, presided. Scouts were thrown out to watch for the arrival of the evening train, but up to 8 o'clock Scofield had not appeared.

"It was the opinion of James H. Green, jun., Scofield's cousin, that a practical joke had been played. He darkly hinted that Scofield might have put up the job himself to seem like a hero in the eyes of the Summit girls. The ladies think it is a base conspiracy to restrict them to the attentions of local admirers, and they did not approve of a prohibitory duty of this kind. It seems that Scofield has at some time or other taken most of them home from church, as well as to the sacred edifices which adorn Summit. His religious tastes were Catholic, but he listened with equal cheerfulness and appreciation to the Methodist preacher, the Rev. Mr. Johns; the Baptist clergyman, the Rev. Dr. Horr; and the rector of the Episcopal Church, the Rev. Dr. Butterworth. He always had a girl with him, and his Sunday demeanour was meek and smooth and silky, and generally edifying.

"The girl he took most often to church, however, was Miss Hetty Tyler, the blonde divinity of the local feed store. Little Minnie Green, Scofield's cousin, artlessly indicated the existing condition of affairs by telling *The World* reporter that 'Willie had been keeping company with Hetty for two or three years, but they had a fight lately and Willie had been taking up with Lidy Swayne.'

"When the coolness sprang up between Scofield and Miss Tyler, it was Miss Swayne who got the oysters over in Adams's restaurant, the ice cream in the bakery, and the delicious soda water from Alec Taylor's handsome fountain. The reporter called upon Miss Tyler to find out what she thought of the letters Scofield and his Uncle James had received. She is a slim, icy girl, in a red waist. She said coldly that she knew nothing about them or about Scofield.

"'Have not your erstwhile relations with Mr. Scofield, which I understand were of a friendly, not to say affectionate nature, recently been rudely shattered?' asked the reporter.

"'I don't know what you mean,' said Miss Tyler, bridling up; 'but he is no relative of mine, and never will be.'

"'What is Mr. Scofield's present occupation?'

"'Loafing mostly, I guess,' said Miss Tyler, with asperity.

"'Aren't you worried over these threats of violence against Mr. Scofield?'

"'Well, I guess not,' said Miss Tyler, with an audible sneer; 'you might see Lidy Swayne about that.'

"'How can I identify Miss Swayne when I see her?'

"'Oh, she's a stumpy girl, with black eyes, and wears her hair hanging round her shoulders.'

"But Miss Swayne was not to be seen. If her heart is lacerated at the threats against Scofield, she only shares in the feelings of 99 per cent. of the Summit girls."

CHAPTER XII.

3500 MILES IN THE TRAIN—PITTSBURGH—WASHINGTON—MR.
BLAINE—THE AMERICAN NAVY—PRESIDENT HARRISON—
WASHINGTON'S HOME—NEW YORK—HOMEWARD BOUND.

Liverpool, April 20th, 1889.

AT Los Angeles I had the outlook before me of 3500 miles in the railway train. A doleful prospect! I chose the Santa Fe route, the least interesting of the five trans-Continental lines, but possessing the merit of keeping one largely out of the snow and frost, for which, after roasting in the Californian sun so long, I had no fancy. Four days and nights across the desert, the dreary tablelands among the Rockies, and the brown parched plains of the Prohibition State of Kansas brought me to Kansas City, on the River Missouri. Thence in a day I reached St. Louis, on the Mississippi, where I treated myself to a day's rest to fortify me for another night and day in the cars. My objective was Pittsburgh, where I was to be the guest of my genial friend Mr. Henry Phipps, who had spent ten weeks with me in California, and preceded me home. Pittsburgh, as all the world knows, is the great centre of the iron and glass industries of Western Pennsylvania. It and its companion, Alleghany City, are most charmingly situated. Two great rivers, the Alleghany and the Monongahela, meet at this point, forming the Ohio, and on the peninsula between the waters, along the sloping banks of the rivers, Pittsburgh and Alleghany City nestle themselves and their joint population of probably 300,000 souls.

This low-lying peninsula is a historic spot. On it, in the pre-Pittian days, the French built Fort Duquesne in their attempt to connect Canada and the Mississippi, and shut in the struggling British Colonies between the forests and the sea. Not to the public buildings or great industrial works of the cities, but to the remains of this fort, was my first visit made.

Fort in the real sense there is none, but amongst the narrow and tortuous streets of what is now the poorest part of Pittsburgh an old ramshackle red-brick house stands as its only surviving relic. The stone which used to adorn the wall, and records name and date, has been removed to the City Hall. It was curious to stand in the midst of great industrious communities and think that little more than a century ago here, amidst boundless forests and howling Indians, the French, in their struggle for colonial empire, boldly planted themselves—the French first and then the British. For of course, despite Braddock's disaster, we omnivorous British captured Fort Duquesne and re-christened it Fort Pitt, transmuted nowadays into Pittsburgh. The scene of Braddock's defeat, where a handful of French and Indians ambushed and destroyed a British force, and where a raw Virginian colonel of militia, known since to all the world as George Washington, first proved what stuff he was made of, is eighteen miles from the city. Then a leafy wilderness, now the seat of the great steel-works of Mr. Carnegie and his partners, it is known still as Braddock. What irony of fate and fame! Alexander's name is perpetuated in Alexandria, and Braddock's in the scene of his shame.

Pittsburgh is the centre of the great region of natural gas, which is tapped at multitudes of wells and conveyed in pipes to the cities. Blast-furnaces are fired with it, and drawing-rooms heated. The commerce and the gain are marvellous, as is indeed the advantage to Pittsburgh in another way. Before the discovery Sheffield was not murkier and dirtier. Now the sun has fairplay, and the city, delivered from soot and smoke, is fair to look upon. The Pittsburgians may pray for gas, more gas, always gas. But it is doubtful whether this wonderful subterranean supply will be of long continuance, for already

MOUNT VERNON. WASHINGTON'S HOME.

the pressure, at least at some of the wells, is diminishing, and Pittsburgh, Heaven help her, may have to condescend to coal again.

After a too brief stay I took the cars again and passed on to Washington. The roadway of this Pennsylvanian railway is excellent, and the running smooth and swift. It is the only line I used of which I can speak in such terms, for the journeying elsewhere is not by progression, but by jerks. The day was fine, the scenery charming. We crossed the Alleghanies, careering along the sides of noble hills and through the recesses of wooded valleys, rounded the wonderful Horse-shoe Bend, and then made our way down the banks of a river, broader and more majestic than the Thames, and quite as lovely. Yet it is but one of the little rivers of this mighty land. They call it the Juanita. I had never heard its name before. At Harrisburg we met Mr. Carnegie, fresh from a great speech he had been delivering to a special session of the Pennsylvania Legislature on the coal and iron industries of the State, with particular reference to differential and preferential rates charged by the Pennsylvanian line. Carried away by his eloquence and the undoubted strength of his facts, the Legislature voted at once for action by the requisite two-thirds majority. Bravo! But now mark the issue. The vote needed, under the law, to be confirmed by a similar vote, which was fixed for two days after. But the railway and the minority organised a country excursion for that day, carried off sufficient of the majority to make a legal vote impossible, and the whole affair ended in legislative smoke. They do strange things in America. If only the standing orders in our Parliament could be modified, what vistas of delight this little incident would open up to British Obstructives.

Our purpose in going round by Washington was to pay our respects to the new President. My readers may remember that on coming out I called on President Cleveland. Whilst I luxuriated in California a peaceful but decisive revolution had been effected. Exit Cleveland; enter Harrison. The nation spoke, and the change was made—simply, legally, most effectively. Would that we king-ridden Europeans could get rid of useless or harmful rulers as easily as our cousins substitute one good man for another!

We first called on Mr. Blaine. He had not arrived at his office, and we were received by his son, Mr. Walker Blaine, who acts as Assistant-Secretary, and whose prompt, suave, and decisive dealing with numerous visitors impressed us favourably with his capacity for business. Whilst we waited the Secretary of State arrived, and we were ushered into his sanctum. I had not seen him since Mr. Cowen and I parted from him and the coaching party at Hexham, in July 1888, leaving them to make their way northward amidst unrespecting Northumbrian rain. Then he looked pale, worn-out, and unwell. Now I was glad to see him looking fresh and hearty, the sickly whiteness of the under-lip replaced by healthy ruddiness, and his whole manner that of one with whom things went well. The general aspect of his face is one of shrewd repose. The white hair rising over a well-developed forehead lends dignity to its appearance; and pleasing manners, a rare but most sweet smile, and a boundless flow of interesting talk, make him a delightful companion. We gossiped for half-an-hour on matters political, literary, and social. One view of his I was sorry to learn. America, he declared, must have a stronger navy. Every section of public opinion demanded it. I am bound to say that so far as my observation went, from New York to California, among Democrats and Republicans alike, that is so. "You English," said the Secretary, "can't wonder at it. Here you are going to spend twenty-one millions extra over a similar policy." Yes, that is the mischief of it. After expending 300 millions in twenty years, our incompetent Naval Authorities declare we have not sufficient navy and guns. They feel bound to spend more. Immediately Russia responds by a resolve to increase her navy, Germany will follow suit, and France, and Italy, and now America; and in the end the relative proportions will remain about the same as at the beginning. Will

THE BED AND ROOM WHERE WASHINGTON DIED.

there ever a statesman arise who will point out to the Christian (?) nations a more excellent way? I mentioned to Mr. Blaine our desire to see the President. "Well, I have an hour's work," said he. "Run off now. Come at one o'clock, and I will walk across with you myself."

At the appointed time we were ushered into the outer room, and found it filled with callers, among whom Mr. Blaine was moving, despatching one after the other with the swift precision only to be attained by a disciplined American politician. My English eyes followed the kaleidoscopic scene with lively curiosity. One incident attracted my especial notice. Mr. Blaine was talking confidentially with General Schenck when his eye, roaming round the room, alighted on a coloured man dressed in broadcloth and with a huge gold watchchain across his ample chest. He was standing shuffling from one foot to the other and uneasily crumpling his billycock in his hand, evidently too embarrassed to take a seat. Mr. Blaine courteously waved him to a chair and went on talking. Then, disregarding many other anxious visitors, he crossed the room, talked, evidently satisfactorily, to his black brother, and dismissed him, smiling all over, with a warm shake of the hand. When we were back in his private room I took the liberty of asking, "Well, and who was your coloured friend?" "Oh," said he, "quite a remarkable man in his way. To begin with, he is, for one of his class, wealthy; then he has the gift of eloquence and of native wit; he makes good speeches, and (with twinkling eye) he can command more votes amongst his people in East Maryland than anybody else." I admired the trained manager of men.

We walked across to the White House, the Secretary laughingly referring to the common charge against him by certain organs in London that he is bellicose and inimical to England. "Here I am in office," he said, "and you can tell your friend the *Times* I am quite prepared to go to immediate war with six or seven of the European States, but (smilingly) not with less." We were immediately introduced to the President, Mr. Blaine preceding us for a moment into the room to smooth our path. We found President Harrison in the same room, at the same desk, and on the same chair occupied four months before by President Cleveland. Thus "Amurath to Amurath succeeds, to Harry Harry," though not by hereditary right. He is a man rather under than over the middle size, well and stoutly built; his hair and beard are fast whitening; his expression indicates kindliness and goodness rather than strength. He welcomed us in soft measured tones, full of the rhythmic intonations and rising inflexions peculiar to the American race. It seemed to me that he looked harassed, careworn, and run down; and I gathered that three months of office-giving and office-refusing had told upon him so that he was anxiously yearning for quiet and rest. Our talk fell upon the past, and the President gave us an interesting description of the manor-houses and modes of life of the old Virginian families, from one of which he sprang. I introduced the name of General Harrison, the king-slayer, mentioning that I had an old copy in black-letter, date 1660, of the Trial of the Regicides.

The President thought that there was no direct descent (which is, I think, correct, since General Tom, if I am not mistaken, left no descendants), but that they were of the same family he thought all but certain; "though to be sure," said he, "there is this against it, that all our Virginian ancestors were high Tories and good Churchmen." I suggested that this general fact was of little moment in fervid times. Cromwell, too, came of a church-going, loyalty-loving race, yet he abased a church and slew a king. Whatever the President's ancestors may have been, he himself is a Puritan of the truest type. I wonder if my readers have read the description of a final scene when he was on the point of leaving his quiet Indiana home to assume his high position. A club of old soldiers, his associates in the Great War, presented him with a costly Bible, on the blank leaves of which were inscribed the names of 130 veterans who have gone from

earth, and the signatures of 121 who participated in the gift. The General was deeply affected. His closing words were these—

"I shall lean upon you and upon that great company of God-fearing people whom I represent. I cannot hope to escape just criticism in the discharge of the enormous and complicated duties which are soon to devolve upon me, but I do hope that I shall escape any fatal error, and that it will appear, when my inadequate and brief work is done, that I have before me, as the pole star of my public life, a patriotic purpose to promote the true glory of our country and the highest good of our people. God bless you every one! May the consolation of this holy book fill your lives with peace, and make the last the best day of all your honourable lives."

These be noble words. Contrast this scene with the first act, the first utterance of the young German Emperor, who, almost ere his father's body was cold, rushes to pen a frantic truculent address, not to the people but to the army, exalting the war-spirit and appealing to the false gods of glory and of fame. Then thank God that if there be warlike autocrats in the world there are peace-loving Presidents too.

We bade President Harrison adieu, feeling that a great nation has for its chief a true man, and devoted the afternoon to a visit to Mrs. Blaine and the young ladies, the latter of whom we were delighted to find fresher and more blooming even than when they were on the coach last year. The family are as yet in a hotel, for Mr. Blaine's own Washington house is let on lease, and the one he has taken was not ready. It is a house of mournful fame, for it is that in which Mr. Seward, Mr. Blaine's great prototype and predecessor, was stabbed on that fatal Good Friday of 1865 when Lincoln was slain. *Absit omen!*

One interesting task remained for us to perform. What lover of liberty visits Washington and does not make a pilgrimage to Washington's home, Washington's grave? We steamed on a sunny morning down the broad Potomac, landed at Mount Vernon, and mounted the wooded hill on which the modest wooden mansion stands. Everything was in trim, cleanly, habitable order, as though the master were about, being kept so by the patriotic subscriptions of citizens of the various States. There was the old-fashioned furniture, the chair he sat on, the flute he played, the sword he wore, the old valise which contained his scanty wardrobe through the gruesome winter at Valley Forge, the bed he died on, the key of the Bastille, which Lafayette sent to him who in all the world was worthiest to possess it. And just below were the old vault where first he lay, and the newer but modest and unpretentious tomb before which annually tens of thousands stand to honour him whose noble distinction it was to be—" First in peace, first in war, and first in the affections of his countrymen."

I forbear detailed description of what has been so often and so well described. And my musings I wrap up in my own soul. Much to me, they were little, I trow, to all the world beside. Of course I found the inevitable Irish Nationalist here, this one engaged in photographing the crowds of visitors. When he mastered my modest identity he was good enough to insist on photographing me in front of the mansion, and presenting me with a much-prized hickory cane grown above the grave. If ever I reach the North Pole I expect to find a Parnellite there.

As we left the bank and slowly moved up the river, the steamer, just as when we arrived, dipped her flag whilst the minute-bell gave forth its mournful voice. Thus do all vessels passing up and down the Potomac pay solemn and poetic tribute to the memory of the Father of the Republic. Say not again that Democracies are deficient in sentiment or forget to be grateful. Thus sang an American poetess forty years ago:—

"Slowly sailing, slowly sailing, hushed the music, mute the mirth,
 Men and maidens standing reverent as on some broad altar's
  hearth.

 . . . .

"Silently before Mount Vernon, silently our boat glides on,
 Hushed its iron heart's deep panting past the Tomb of Washington;
 Truest, worthiest act of worship that degenerate earth now knows,
 Inmost soul here recognising all the mighty debt she owes.

" Oh, my country, art thou paling—losing all thy young day's glow?
Can'st thou lose thy first love's glory, and thy hero's worth still
    know?
Patriot hearts, do doubts still haunt you, threatening thoughts come
    crowding on?
Sail with me down broad Potomac, past the Tomb of Washington;

" Feel the impress of his greatness stamped upon the Nation's heart,
See each manly brow uncovered, lovely lips in awe apart;
Fear not while this reverence lingers with its clear, warm, hallowing
    light;
This must fade from brow and bosom ere can come our country's
    night."

Next day saw me in New York in the midst of pleasant associates. I spent my only available evening dining with my good friend Mr. Buckley at the Union League, the famous Republican Club of New York. On the Saturday Mr. Buckley and Mr. and Mrs. Carnegie saw me aboard. The good ship ploughed her way at the rate of twenty-two land miles an hour, cutting a hole 3000 miles long, fifty-six feet broad, and twenty-four feet deep, through the patient, peaceful waters of the Atlantic, and in six days nineteen hours the anchor of the *Umbria* rested in the mud of the Mersey.

Here my gossip ends. One parting confession let me make. I am, I suppose, the only Englishman of leisure who has spent many months in travelling right across the American Continent and back without seeing either Niagara Falls, or the Yellowstone Park, or the Yosemite Valley, or the Colorado Canon! My unapologetic explanation is' this. I went solely to seek health and warmth and the sun. I found Paradise, and I stayed there. If my explanation be not sufficient, then write me down— An Ass.

www.ingramcontent.com/pod-product-compliance
Lightning Source LLC
Chambersburg PA
CBHW030314170426
43202CB00009B/996